The Past in the Present

The Past in the Present

THE NATIONAL MUSEUM OF DENMARK

The Past in the Present

Copyright: The National Museum of Denmark and the authors 2015
Editor: *Bodil Bundgaard Rasmussen*
Design: *Freddy Pedersen*
Layout production: *Narayana Press*
Typeset Bembo and printed on Galerie Art Silk

ISBN 978-87-89438-09-2
Translation: Dan Marmorstein p. 11-112.

Published with financial support from:

Dronning Margrethes og Prins Henriks Fond
Generalkonsul Gösta Enboms Fond
Grosserer Emil Schous Legat
H.P. Hjerl-Hansen Mindefondet for Dansk Palæstinaforskning

Contents

Preface

A few years ago, the Collection of Classical and Near Eastern Antiquities in the National Museum of Denmark received a small package from Germany. It turned out to contain a CD with a piece of music, "The Dream of Seikilos", composed by Istvan Horvath-Thomas. It was inspired by and based on the hymn on the so-called Seikilos stele in the National museum, i.e. a sepulchral column with an epitaph and below this a Greek inscription in the form of a short poem most unusually accompanied by musical notes. The stele has been studied intensively in recent years by several international scholars and has been included in a number of international special exhibitions as a prime example of ancient music. Moreover, the stele was included in a British television production on the history of music.

The Seikilos stele – and the many roles it has played in the transmission of knowledge of the Ancient world – perfectly exemplifies the huge potential of the Collection of Classical and Near Eastern Antiquities to transmit and transform the past to contemporary society. At the same time it demonstrates the degree to which we can continue even today to find inspiration in Classical Antiquity. This endeavor is at the back of the articles gathered in the present volume, which were written by researchers of the National Museum and colleagues from other Academic institutions.

We are thus delighted to include the publication of one of the first groups of ancient portraits acquired by King Frederik V, which found their way to Denmark, written by Mette Moltesen, former curator at the Ny Carlsberg Glyptotek. We are indebted also to the former Keeper of "Greek and Roman" in the British Museum, Dr. Dyfri Williams, for two contributions. Dr. Williams was a guest re-searcher at the National Museum's research programme "Pots, Potters and Society in Ancient Greece" (2008-2014) that was launched thanks to generous support by Consul General Gösta Enbom's Foundation. One concerns the discovery that two fragments of a terracotta mould from Tarento in Southern Italy that are kept in the British Museum and in the Danish National Museum, respectively, join to form a mould for an exquisite female head. Dyfri Williams' second contribution is a meticulous study of fragments of a Greek pinax, i.e. a burial plaque, acquired

Sepulchral stele erected by Seikilos, an otherwise unknown Greek. Engraved on the stele is a grave epitaph and below that a poem with musical notes between the lines. On of the very few surviving inscriptions with musical notation known from the Greco-Roman world. Marble, height 61 cm. 1st cent. AD. Classical and Near Eastern Antiquities, the National Museum of Denmark.

in Athens in 1863 at the time of the inauguration of the Danish Prince Vilhelm as King Georg I of Greece. Professor emeritus, dr. phil. Henrik Thrane contributes an article on the expedition by the National Museum to Luristan in Iran, in which he participated in his capacity as curator in the department of Danish Prehistory in the National Museum. Anne Haslund Hansen and Peter Pentz deal with previously unpublished finds in the Collection of Classical and Near Eastern Antiquities and John Lund and the undersigned highlight personalities and events connected to the establishment of the collection.

I wish to express my warmest thanks for support to the present publication to Dronning Margrethes og Prins Henriks Fond, Generalkonsul Gösta Enboms Fond, Grosserer Emil Schous Legat and H.P. Hjerl-Hansen Mindefondet for Dansk Palæstinaforskning.

Bodil Bundgaard Rasmussen

The poem and melody on the column:

While you're alive, shine man,
don't be the least bit blue.
Life's for a little span;
Time demands its due.

ho - son   zēs   fai - - nu/ mē - den

ho - lōs   sy - ly - pu __/ pros o - li - gon e - sti to

zēn __/ to te - los ho khro - nos a - pai - tei. ____

(Poem: M.L. West, Ancient Greek Music, Oxford 1992.
Melody: Carsten Høeg, Musik og digtning i byzantinsk kristendom. København 1955.)

Among Humans and Quadrupeds
An Egyptian Mummy in the Kunstkammer

Anne Haslund Hansen

The Royal Kunstkammer was a showplace for nature's multiplicity and for mankind's capabilities. In one room after the next, the visitor could be surprised and amused, glancing at the exquisite showcases with peculiarities from near and far, from both present and past. One of the most sensational objects in the collection was an ancient Egyptian mummy in its coffin.

According to the categories of the Kunstkammer this mummy was an archaeological artefact that could be studied as an historic relic, replete with a coffin – decorated with hieroglyphs – linen wrappings and religious symbolism. At the same time, the mummy was also a piece of scientific material holding information on anatomy, human specimens and medicine.

By the means of contemporary sources this article examines the various interpretations of the mummy that have been put forth. Five different aspects of the mummy are considered: its staging as a showpiece, as an antiquity and as a polyfaceted object of the natural sciences. Furthermore the article presents new information on the acquisition of the mummy and coffin, and its appearance in the famous 17th century scholarly work, *Oedipus Aegyptiacus*. Finally a short Egyptological description of the coffin is given.

THE ENVOY AND THE MUMMY

The mummy and its wooden coffin which are presently kept in the Collection of Classical and Near Eastern Antiquities are among the earliest Egyptian acquisitions in the Kunstkammer, fig. 1. Accordingly, it is listed in the oldest of the extant inventories of the collection, which was completed in the year 1674. The concise description reads: *A large mumia, laid out in a coffin, which has been formed according to the shape of the body and covered with Egyptian script.*[1]

The inventory provides no further clue about when or how the mummy came to be included in the Kunstkammer. However, part of the answer to these questions can be found in a later source, namely the *Museum Regium,* the title of two successive catalogues of the Kunstkammer collections. The first of these

Fig. 1.
Coffin with mummy. Painted wood. Length: 195 cm. c. 400-300 BC
Inv. No. AAa2. Photo: Peter Danstrøm, The National Museum of Denmark.

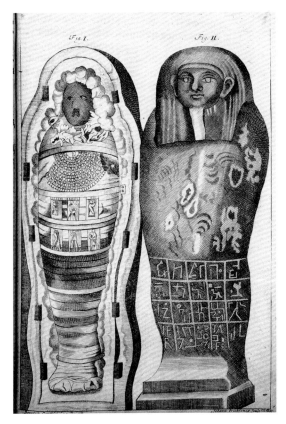

Fig. 2.
Rendering of coffin and mummy in Museum Regium, 1696,
Tab. I.

Fig. 3.
Rendering in Museum Regium, 1710, Tab. I. Compared with the
reproduction in the 1696 edition, the area around the lower part
of the coffin appears more indistinct, while the hieroglyphs on the
side have now become visible.

Fig. 4.
Peder Charisius (1608-85), Painting by Karel van Mander, 1670. The Museum of National History at Frederiksborg Castle, A 2896.

was published in 1696 and the second in 1710, both volumes having been written in Latin, the scientific *lingua franca* of its day.[2] Both editions of the *Museum Regium* contain a description of the mummy and an engraving, figs. 2 and 3. In the *Museum Regium* from 1710, we are informed that the mummy was obtained for the Kunstkammer by a certain Petrus Jonas Carisius, King Frederik III's *Belgas legatus*,[3] fig. 4.

In the years from 1651 to 1669, this Peder Charisius (1608–85), was King Frederik III's envoy in The Hague in "the States General" of the Netherlands.[4] Charisius contributed to the collections of the Kunstkammer on several occasions. During his period of sojourn as *Belgas legatus* in the important commercial centre of The Hague, he had the opportunity to purchase a number of objects for the king, who then had them added to the Kunstkammer. Later on, after he returned to Denmark, Charisius donated his private collection of rarities to the Kunstkammer, now under the protection of King Christian V (regent 1670-1699), but the exact year of the donation is not known.[5]

The mummy has previously been assigned, variously, to Charisius's acquisitions made on behalf of Frederik III and to Charisius's private collection.[6] There is much to indicate that Charisius was still in possession of his own private collection in 1674, at which time the mummy first appears in the Kunstkammer' inventory. In his description of the sights of Copenhagen, published in 1673, Holger Jacobæus (1650-1701), author of the 1696 edition of *Museum Regium,* sets forth a description of *both* the Kunstkammer' and Charisius's collection.[7] Whereas when referring to Charisius's collection, mention is made *only* of an *Infans 5 mensium, Mumia,* which means to say a child mummy, the Kunstkammer can boast of a *Mumia capsæ inclusa cum Hieroglyphicis ægyptiacis,* which is an almost literal re-rendering of the text from the 1674 inventory. If we are to put our faith in Jacobæus, then, it is clear that the mummy already belonged to the Kunstkammer *before* Charisius's collection was annexed.

Jacobæus's interest in Charisius and his collection was far from casual. On the very day Jacobæus visited the Kunstkammer and made a note of its rarities, he was accompanied, in fact — by Peder Charisius.

ATHANASIUS KIRCHER AND THE DUTCH CONNECTION

The acquisition history of the Kunstkammer mummy can be traced even further back than Charisius. The three-volume work, *Oedipus Aegyptiacus*, 1652-54 contains a series of hitherto unnoticed renderings and a description of this coffin, fig. 5 (see H, I and K). In the text the coffin is said to belong to the collection of a merchant from Amsterdam named H. van Werle, and in all likelihood it is directly from here that Charisius acquired it.[8]

The author of *Oedipus Aegyptiacus* was Athanasius Kircher (1602-1680) a learned Jesuit, born near Fulda, and residing in Rome since 1633. Kircher was undisputedly the 17th century's greatest authority on ancient Egypt, and *Oedipus* was the first of several works on the religion of this ancient culture. Kircher was a collector himself, and his Museum Kircherianum was one of the most renowned cabinets of curiosities of its time. Antiquities played a vital role in Kircher's scientific studies. Many of the necessary sources were secured via an extensive scholarly network. Bartholdus Nihusius, a Catholic clergyman in Amsterdam, transmitted the three images of the coffin from Van Werle's collection to Kircher. The images in the 1652-54 *Oedipus* add yet two more significant decades to the documented history of the mummy — as compared to the oldest known Danish sources of 1673/74.

THE STAGED MUMMY

The Kunstkammer was a magnet for the remarkable and the rare. By virtue of its ancient and remote origins, the Egyptian mummy could easily come to be a genuine rarity on a par with *Elephant Teeth, Coconuts* and a *Bacchus of copper.* But even in the very manner of the mummy's display, its curious properties were emphasised. The coffin has been exhibited in an upright position. On one of the

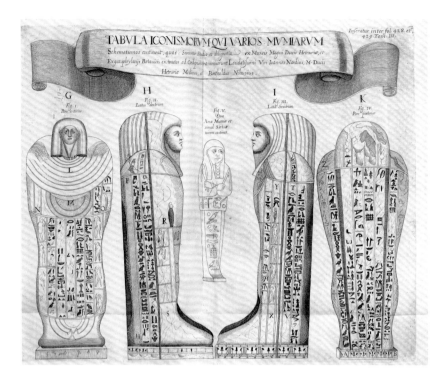

Fig. 5.
Rendering of the coffin in Oedipus Aegyptiacus, 1654. Photo: Bodleian Library.

lengthways sides, three solid hinges were fastened, while on the opposite side, there was a hasp for keeping the coffin closed, fig. 6. Moreover, a heavy wooden bar was mounted at the base so that the coffin's lid could be moved freely. Several clues suggest a frequent use of this rather extensive device. The hasp's exterior compass manifests itself visibly as a deep circular groove in the wood – made from wear and tear. A large portion of the coffin's lid bears the marks of years of use. When the coffin was opened before the curious eye of the visitor the wrapped mummy could be observed, meticulously fastened with straps of gilded leather. The date of the mounting of the hinges and hasps is not known, but with respect to the apparent craftsmanship, it does not seem implausible to assume that these features might have been added at the end of the seventeenth century. If we compare the coffin with the plate found in *Museum Regium* 1696, it can be further ascertained that the mummy was already fitted with straps at that time. On the other hand, there are no traces of the hinges, but this might be due to considerations about the illustration's clarity.

A similar and even more elaborate staging existed in the British Museum's exhibition rooms of the mid-18th century. Here one of the museum's Egyptian

Fig. 6.
The open coffin. Lid and
trough are attached with
the aid of three large hinges,
probably dating from the late
17ᵗʰ century. The mummy
has been fastened with bands.
Inv. No. AAa2. Photo: Peter
Danstrøm, The National
Museum of Denmark.

mummy cases was mounted on a spinning device that enabled the visitors to view the case from all sides. The mounting no longer exists, but is known from written accounts.[9] A coffin in Grenoble, acquired in the late 18ᵗʰ century, is equipped with hinges and a handle for opening the coffin lid, and also wheels for easy transportation.[10]

The coffin's mountings and marked wear embody a most eloquent tale of the decided staging of Egyptian rarities in the early European collections. A staging that served to underline 17ᵗʰ and 18ᵗʰ century perceptions of the esoteric Egyptians and their peculiar funerary cult, while at the same time it anticipates the 19ᵗʰ century's preference for emotional tableaux with live specimens of exotic peoples or vivid mock-ups of long lost cultures.

THE ANTIQUARIAN MUMMY

The world of the antiquaries was a colourful admixture of Latin apophthegms, unearthed relics and heads in plaster. It was a variegated world, which subsumed such now severed disciplines as archaeology, art history, philology and history. Until the middle of the nineteenth century, when Egyptology became an independent discipline, the study of ancient Egypt belonged to the domain of the antiquarians. The sources in this area were the classical writers and the ancient remains, in the form of both the actual relics and the description of monuments in Egypt. It was not until the decipherment of J.-F. Champollion in 1822, that the Egyptian hieroglyphs could function as source material. The antiquarian exploration of Egypt was especially concentrated around the Egyptian imagery and the religious conceptions conjectured to be seated behind these.

The antiquarian view with regard to the Kunstkammer's mummy is manifested distinctly in the inventories and in the *Museum Regium*. In the inventory drawn up in 1690, the mummy is expounded as *A large mummy, laid out in a coffin, which has been formed according the shape of the body and covered with Egyptian script, [and] which can be assumed to be one of the Egyptian Pharaohs.*[11] This somewhat pompous interpretation is elaborated further in *Museum Regium* 1710 with the additional explanation that the mummy's ornamentation is so *magnifico,* that it must have been a person of the highest rank.[12] The fact that in reality, the mummy is that of a private person and not a pharaoh was something that the seventeenth and eighteenth centuries had only severely limited possibilities for determining – the knowledge of the primary sources was all too fragmentary.

In the inventory drawn up in 1737, the emphasis was transferred to a religious interpretation of the coffin. *A large mummy, wrapped – and elaborately ornamented – with old Egyptian hieroglyphs, laid in a coffin made in the shape of the body, bearing a resemblance to Isis's image, made of sycamore wood.* The mentioning of the Egyptian goddess Isis comes as no surprise. Isis was one of the most prominent deities in the seventeenth and eighteenth centuries' Egyptian pantheon. This was the consequence of the strong influence from the classical writers and from the Roman pantheon, of which Isis had become a part.[13]

A considerable portion of the description in *Museum Regium* deals with the decoration of the mummy. The two plates in *Museum Regium* 1696 and 1710 show that the decoration originally consisted of a broad collar and six small plaquettes. During the present examination a single plaquette has been retrieved, which was rolled up inside one of the coffin's tapholes, fig. 7. This piece is executed in painted plaster on cloth, otherwise known as cartonnage, and represents the baboon-headed divinity Hapy, one of the so-called "four sons of Horus" who protected the dead. If we compare the extant plaquette with the engravings in *Museum Regium*, it is the edition from 1710 which is the more accurate in its rendition. Four of the six

Fig. 7.
Part of the decoration from the mummy. The ape-headed deity, Hapy is mummiform, and is shown carrying a piece of cloth for use in the embalming process. Cartonnage, painted plaster on linen. Inv. No. AAa2. Photo: The National Museum of Denmark.

plaquettes on the plate appear to be almost identical and ostensibly constitute a complete set of the four sons of Horus who, in addition to Hapy, consist of Duamutef – with a falcon's head, Imsety – with the human head and Qebehsenuef – with the head of a jackal. It is quite certain that the two remaining pieces, placed, respectively, uppermost at the right and at the bottom on the left, also represent funerary deities, most likely the goddesses Isis and Nephthys. In *Museum Regium,* the six depictions of divinities are not altogether incorrectly perceived as protective divinities. Somewhat less successful, by today's standards, is the reading of the collar's stylised floral bands, the thirteen semi-circles of which are set into connection with such weighty themes as heavenly bodies and the wandering of the soul.[14] The complex interpretation is characteristic of the period's predilection for religious and mystically coloured readings of Egyptian culture.

Owing to its affinity with archaeology, the antiquarian investigation also displayed an interest in topics such as archaeological context and the comparative study of antiquities. In *Museum Regium,* reference is made to two contemporary authors, both of whom offered accounts of mummies and where they are found, namely Athanasius Kircher (only in the 1696 edition) and Jean de Thévenot. There is no mention of any particular work by Kircher, and the reference must therefore encompass all his works on Egypt. Thévenot's *Rejseberetning* [Travel Account], as it is merely referred to in *Museum Regium,* cannot be anything other than his *Relation d'un Voyage fait au Levant,* which was published in 1665, and remained a popular reference work well into the 18th century. Both of these authors speak about the abundant burial places in the Memphite region, near modern-day Cairo, which supplied the seventeenth century's European travellers with souvenirs, ranging from complete mummies to diminutive amulets.[15] It was the mummies, however, that constituted the area's main attraction and frequently, the area was actually called *the plain of mummies.*

It was not before the beginning of the nineteenth century that the systematic collecting of ancient Egyptian artefacts was initiated in Middle and Upper Egypt.

THE MUMMY AS A NATURAL SPECIMEN

The descriptions in the inventories and in the two editions of *Museum Regium* delineate what is clearly an antiquarian portrait of the mummy. If, on the other hand, we turn our gaze toward the actual placement of the mummy in the classification of the Kunstkammer an entirely different and, as far as the present is concerned, more unexpected picture comes into view.

In *Museum Regium,* the objects are divided up into two groups: those which are of nature's world, *naturalia* – and those which have been artificially processed or man-made, *artificialia,* fig. 8. Whereas the rest of the collection's antiquities have been categorised as *artificialia,* the mummy – on the contrary – is included among the natural specimens. In this vein, it takes up the central role in the very first section, which is entitled *On humans and quadrupeds,* fig. 9. The classification, which is followed also by birds and fish, is drawn up according to the ancient system of Aristotle, a system which continued to be valid until the taxonomy of Carl von Linnaeus became widely accepted. The mummy's prominent place among the natural items was additionally enunciated with an introductory pictorial vignette, fig. 9. Behind the accentuated 'M' in 'Mumia' the mummy's opened coffin can be seen, while the centre of the vignette is taken up by a showcase with a smaller mummy, supposedly the child mummy, *Mumia Ægyptiaca minor,* which was also part of the collection.[16] Finally, the marked interest in the mummy also

MUSÉUM REGIUM

SEU

CATALOGUS

Rerum tam naturalium, quàm artificialium,

QUÆ

IN BASILICA BIBLIOTHECÆ
AUGUSTISSIMI DANIÆ NORVEGIÆq;

MONARCHÆ

CHRISTIANI QVINTI

Hafniæ affervantur,
Defcriptus
Ab

OLIGERO JACOBÆO,

Med. & Phil. Prof. Regio,

CUM PRIVILEGIO.

HAFNIÆ,
Literis Reg. Celf. Typogr. JOACHIMI SCHMETGEN,
ANNO M. DC. XCVI.

SECTIO I.
DE
Homine & Qvadrupedibus.

UMIA ÆGYPTIACA (*Tab. I. Fig. I.*) pedum qvinq; longitudine, carbaſo ſubtili & telâ varia undiq; involuta. In faſciis circumjectis figuræ qvædam peculiares conſpiciuntur & characteresHieroglyphici. Limbi circulares, pectus inprimis veſtientes, ex colorum diverſorum orbiculis & figuris aliis aſſuti ſunt, auroq; hinc inde illiti.

    CAPSA ſeu repoſitorium, (*Tab. I. Fig. II.*) cui incluſa eſt Mumia goſſypio hinc inde tecta, ex ligno concavo oblongo, craſſo admodum & coloris ſubflavi, ac in partes binas diviſo, ad ſimilitudinem Mumiæ accedit, & parte ſuperiore capitis humani figuram exprimit; inferiore verò, & qvidem anticâ, notas & characteres peculiares, vetuſtate ferè exeſos. Mumiæ tales ab Ægyptiis olim inprimis confectæ, & funera medicata *Plinio* appellatæ, voce Perſicâ, pro cadaveribus exſiccatis ſumuntur & certâ ratione conditis, qvæ ſub ſtructuris Pyramidum vel in cryptis aliis ſubterraneis apud Ægyptios olim condebantur. De mumiis, præter alios, eruditè *Athanaſius Kircкerus* & in Itinerario ſuo *Thevenotius.*

    MUMIA ÆGYPTIACA minor, pedum trium longitudine, pannis variis involuta & faſciis circumligata.

    MUMIA DANICA. Licet enim inter deperdita Mumiæ veræ à *Pancirollo* habeantur, à recentioribus tamen, ſucceſſu haud diſpari, ars condiendi cadavera exculta eſt, qvâ inclaruère inprimis hoc ſeculo *Bilſius, Boylèus, Blankardus,* alii.

    FOETUS Lapideſactus. (*Tab. XI. Fig. II.*) Mirandum hunc fœtum ſpatio viginti octo annorum mulier Agendici Senonum in Gallia geſtavit, qvæ *Columba Charria* dicta, ſartoris uxor. Diſſecto utero, portentoſâ demum mole gypſeâ eductus eſt fœtus Anno 1582, membris bene conformatis, niſi qvod ultra modum induruerant. Spectatum diu Agendici, tranſiit demum corpuſculum ad mercatorem Pariſienſem primarium, hinc ab aurifabro & gemmario *Giliberto Vautron* Venetias delatum, ac tandem ex Italia anno 1653. ad Auguſtiſſimum Daniæ Regem FRIDERICUM III, qvi inter rariora Muſei

             A2   hujus

Fig. 9.
Description of the mummy in Museum Regium, 1696. At the top of the page is a selection of objects within the category of Humans and quadrupeds. In the right margin, there is a hand-written note that mentions Charisius.

manifested itself through its visual rendering. As one of the few objects in the volume, it was allotted its very own plate, figs. 2 and 3.

The mummy's place among the *naturalia* was not exclusively reserved to the *Museum Regium's* scientific reasoning. The inventories and the actual physical exhibition also assigned the mummy to the world of nature.

In the Kunstkammer classification, the mummy was first and foremost a dead and preserved person and only in the next consideration was it an historic relic of ancient Egypt. In the catalogue is also encountered a *Mumia danica*, a preserved body found in Danish soil.[17] The mummy as a natural specimen is also to be seen in one of *Museum Regium's* closest parallels, the catalogue of the collection at the castle in Gottorp, *Gottorffische Kunst=Kammer,* from 1666. Adam Olearius (1603-1671), the author of the catalogue, divides the objects up into those that were of *die Natur* and those that were made by *künstliche Hände*. The Egyptian mummy, one of which, of course, was also kept in Gottorp, was placed last in the group of natural objects along with a non-Egyptian mummy as well as three ancient artefacts – a vessel, a lamp and a glass bottle, all of which were set into connection with funerals and funeral rites.[18] Through the means of this coupling, Olearius managed to suggest a cultural-historic approach to a scientific object, in much the same way that Jacobæus did with the Kunstkammer mummy 30 years later.

THE MEDICINAL MUMMY

In the 17th and 18th centuries Egyptian mummies also found uses in medical treatment.[19] In the catalogue from Gottorp, for example, Olearius recounts that the mummies *mit grossen Nutzen in Artzneyen können gebrauchet werden/wie man dann auch fast in allen wohlbestalten Apotecken etliche Stücke darvon findet.*[20]

The role of the Egyptian mummies in European medicine was already well-established in the sixteenth century. The very word *mummy* stems from the Persian *mumia*, which means bitumen or asphalt. Originally, the word covered – in its meaning – a naturally occurring tar-like product, to which medicinal qualities were attributed. The mummies that were discovered in Egypt had accumulations of a *mumia*-like material, after which they were named. The accumulations stem from the mummification process and are often concentrated in the mummy's abdominal cavity. Especially in the first millennium BC, large quantities of both resin and bitumen were used during the mummification process. More recent investigations of mummies indicate that resin has been the most predominant substance, while bitumen could also be used together with resin or, in certain instances, by itself.[21]

Naturally occurring *mumia* was a commodity in demand. Eventually, the Egyptian mummies also came to form part of the supply. The use of *mumia* also included, to a certain extent, the mummy's body itself, which due to the mummification could also have a bitumen-like appearance. As a drug, *mumia* was used in powdered form. It was applied externally and was also ingested, and was regarded as a universal remedy. The complex notions related to the *mumia* powder's effect were conjoined with the mummy as a preserved corpus: herein dwelled intrinsic magical and healing powers, which could be of benefit to the ailing patient.

With the ambiguous use of the word *mumia,* a certain linguistic confusion arose. Accordingly, it is not always clear whether the sources mentions *mumia* which has been collected naturally or about *mumia* that has been taken from mummies. Nor is it always clear whether allusion is being made solely to accumulations *on* or *inside* the mummy or if what is being referred to has to do with the body of the mummy itself. And finally, is it not always clear whether it is *mumia* from Egyptian mummies or from other corpses, often executed criminals.[22] The sources testify to several variants of *mumia,* some more sought after than others, fig. 10. The discerning customer could ensure himself the right product by demanding *mumia vera aegyptiaca,* real Egyptian mummy. However, mummies could survive in even the most exposed of places. During the 17th and 18th centuries a pharmacy in Lübeck had an Egyptian mummy set out as advertisement.[23]

It is puzzling that in *Museum Regium,* Jacobæus only mentions the Persian origin of the word *mumia,* while he does not delve further into the mummies' relation to medicine, especially insofar as he was undoubtedly aware of the phe-

Fig. 10.
Drawer with "Mumie" in the category of medical resins. From the intact pharmacy of l'Hôtel-Dieu (built 1750-1763), Carpentras, Provence. Photo: The Author.

nomenon and, as a matter of fact, had already in 1677 taken note of an especially well-supplied pharmacy in Dresden, *where a good many mumiæ and other rarities could be obtained*.[24]

The use of *mumia* did not fully subside before the 19th century, but throughout its history as a drug it served as the object of considerable debate in the medical sciences with regard to its qualities and effects – or shortcomings.

THE ANATOMICAL MUMMY

In 1826, while the Kunstkammer was being dissolved and the collections had to be reorganised, the mummy and the coffin were described anew: *Bands with painted Egyptian figures had been applied everywhere; but these have been removed in connection with the anatomical examinations that were carried out quite some time ago, of which on the one side of the head and on the feet there are recognisable traces*.[25] This passage constitutes what is presently the sole source telling of an anatomical study of the Kunstkammer mummy. The description of the mummy's original appearance appears to be based on the depiction in *Museum Regium*. The *painted Egyptian figures* must, then, refer to the broad collar and the six plaquettes. The direct traces of the anatomical examination make their appearance as *negative imprints*, of a kind, on the mummy, fig. 6. The head, especially, has suffered damage. Whereas in 1826, there was evidently a certain section remaining intact, at the present time, only part of the back of the head can be located. Already on the engravings in *Museum Regium*, however, the wrappings around the face appear to be in disarray. What was not mentioned in 1826 were the rather striking probe marks, which are visible as two oval holes in the upper part of the body. On the mummy's left side, the bone of the arm is even exposed. There are also single instances of smaller holes found elsewhere. It cannot be determined whether these holes also stem from the same examinations, but this seems highly probable. Without offering any precise dating, the aforementioned quotation aids us in placing the investigation of the mummy somewhere between 1696/1710, when it was delineated in *Museum Regium*, and at a time which was already *quite some time ago* in 1826. The middle of the eighteenth century might be a possibility.

Anatomical investigations of Egyptian mummies were especially prominent in the eighteenth and nineteenth centuries. The investigations often turned out as dissections of the corpse and were conducted at the universities or under the auspices of learned societies. It is difficult to conjecture about the number of mummies that were subjected to such examinations. But if we are speaking about Europe on the whole, it is possible to assert that the quantity might have been as many as a several hundred. This tally is rendered all the more difficult, however, by the fact that not all of these investigations eventually found their way into printed sources. The descriptions that are known, above and beyond the purely anatomical observations, often show great interest in embalming technique, especially in the light of information found in the classical sources, most prominently Herodotus.[26]

From Danish sources we know of a description of a typical eighteenth century examination. It was carried out in December 1781 at the University's *Natur-Theater* on Nørregade in Copenhagen. The author of the report, who was also the leading figure in the examination, was zoologist Morten Thrane Brünnich (1723-1803).[27] The mummy, which was placed on view, came from King Frederik V's expedition to Arabia in 1761-67, also known as the Carsten Niebuhr Expedition. Other mummies acquired on the same expedition, found their way into the Kunstkammer. Here, however, they were now registered as antiques and not as natural specimens. Two of the mummies from the aforementioned expedition were sent to Göttingen and to Kiel, for purposes of being subjected to similar examinations.[28]

Brünnich's description treats the coffin as well as the mummy's outer appearance, the bindings and at last, the body itself. The description is additionally supplied with a plate that illustrates different phases of the examination's course, fig. 11. The mummy's decoration consists of pieces of cartonnage as did the Kunstkammer mummy. In order to determine material composition of this decoration, Brünnich exposes fragments of these pieces to water, chemicals and fire. The greater part of the decoration, however, survived the tests and are now to be found in the Collection of Classical and Near Eastern Antiquities. The mummy wrappings received a great deal of attention, which is also made apparent on the illustrative plate. The inner layers of wrappings were coloured by something that Brünnich calls *Mummy-Matter*. What is meant by this, in all probability, is the resin or asphalt which were utilised in the mummification process. Certain salt-like deposits were investigated very directly, namely with the aid of the sense faculty of taste. They *tasted like urine*. When the mummy was subsequently laid so bare that its gender could be determined, Brünnich was disappointed to find *nothing at the spot ... except a small opening of the pelvis*. The sought after body parts, however, were found to be torn from the body and, as Brünnich writes, this tiny wrapped body part *convinced everybody that the mummy belonged to the male sex*. Proof of this is seen on the plate's fig. 6.

The proper anatomical investigation of the mummy was ushered in by sawing open the skull. The internal parts of the body could only be identified with difficulty. Certain areas were found empty, while others were filled with *Mummy-Matter*. It proved to be impossible to separate the legs and arms completely from the wrappings. For this reason, they had to be sawed through before they could be examined.

As it comes to light in Brünnich's description, the examination of the mummy proved to be very destructive. In an overview of the university's collection of

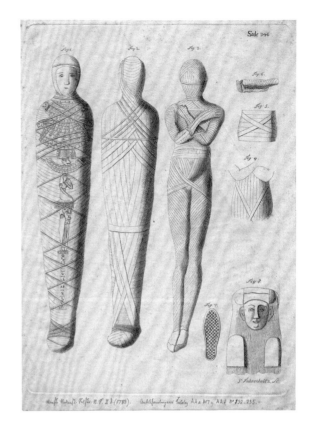

Fig. 11.
Mummy examined by
M. T. Brünnich in 1781.
Fig. 4-6 show details of the
wrappings. From Viden-
skabernes Selskabs Skrifter
II 1783.

natural objects, published in 1782, the year after the aforementioned event, there is a laconic reference to *the head and some parts of the large Egyptian mummy.*[29] In order to have their questions pertaining to anatomy and the art of embalming elucidated, however, eighteenth century scientists did not have many possibilities from which to choose other than a traditional dissection. It was not until much later that gentler methods of X-raying and scanning were put into use.

In comparison with Brünnich's thorough examination in 1781, whatever *anatomical investigations* were performed on the Kunstkammer mummy must be characterised as being of a very limited scope. However, there can be no doubt that any anatomical research, however extensive it might or might not have been, points toward the designation with which the mummy was already bestowed upon its arrival in the Kunstkammer. Ancient or not, the mummy was first and foremost a specimen that belonged among *Humans and quadrupeds.*

Together, description and documentation form the cornerstone in the treatment of archaeological remains. When mummy and coffin were described in *Museum Regium* 1696 and 1710, this was based on the scientific tools and references that were considered to be relevant and reliable at the time. In this respect, the past does not differentiate itself from the present. The difference is to be found in the much greater degree of familiarity with the original sources of which the present day's Egyptological discipline can boast and, of course, derive advantage from.

A typological examination of the coffin is based on the coffin's shape and decoration. The humanoid coffin has two important characteristics. Below the feet a rectangular form can be seen, as if the coffin is mounted on a pedestal. The back of the trough has a back pillar, a raised oblong area running down the centre. These two features are characteristic of Egyptian coffins in the period between 700-300 BC.

The coffin's decoration, unfortunately, is now in very poor condition. At the areas that are best preserved, the coffin is very dark and appears, in all probability, to have been painted black, while the decoration was done in yellow. Around the headpiece, there are remnants of yellow stripes, which originally covered the entire area. On the base, there are remnants of a decorative frieze with three hieroglyphs in a repeated pattern, forming the common phrase *all power and life* (for the deceased). The frieze is only preserved on the underside. The coarsely hewn interior of the lid and trough are entirely devoid of decoration.

Today, the renderings from Athanasius Kircher, fig. 5, give the best impression of the original decoration of the coffin. From these it is evident that it was covered with inscriptions on the front as well as the sides and back. The bands of hieroglyphic text appear to have been combined with small vignettes showing standing deities. A floral broad collar has covered the upper torso – a decorative element often seen on Egyptian coffins.

The two engravings from *Museum Regium* show only the front of the coffin, figs. 2-3. Only singular hieroglyphic signs can be detected and as well as some rough indications of the overall decorative programme, most prominently on the 1696 edition. Both reproductions (1696 and 1710) seem to show that the decoration of the lid was already in a very bad state, and perhaps therefore not included in Kircher's documentation.

The differences between the method of rendering in Kircher and in *Museum Regium* are very noticeable. In Kircher's version, an almost complete and very detailed rendering of the coffin's decoration is seen, and the emphasis lies clearly on the inscriptions. In *Museum Regium* the focus has shifted more towards the physical appearance. The wooden roughness and massive size of the coffin has come forth, and it is now possible to look inside the coffin itself and study the mummy's form and condition of preservation.

The hieroglyphic inscriptions on the coffin are today very fragmented. Best preserved is a band running along the sides of the coffin and smaller sections on the underside of the trough. Inscriptions of Egyptian coffins and sarcophagi consist of excerpts from religious texts and offering prayers as well as a specification of the name, kinship and titles of the dead. On the basis of the preserved text, it has been possible to identify the name of the person as *Wah-ib-Re, son of Udja-Hor, born of Shep*[…], fig. 12. The name *Wah-ib-Re* was borne by the kings

Fig. 12.
Along the sides and back of the coffin, there are remnants of inscriptions. The segment shows the name of the deceased, Wah-ib-Re. Inv. No. AAa2. Photo: The National Museum of Denmark.

Notes

1. Quoted from Liisberg, 1867, 155.
2. The author of *Museum Regium* 1696 was Holger Jacobæus, whereas Johannes Laverentzen took charge of the revised edition from 1710.
3. *Museum Regium* 1710, 1. The same information is notated in the margin of the National Museum's copy of *Museum Regium* 1696, 1, see fig. 2.
4. *Dansk Biografisk Leksikon*, 3rd edition, 3, 217-218.
5. Liisberg, 1897, 64-65 and 113-14. A document dating from 1683, written by Charisius' son, makes it clear that the transfer took place a number of years *before* the date of this document.
6. Liisberg considers the mummy to be part of Charisius' private collection, Liisberg, 1897, 113, while Gundestrup assigns the mummy to the period under King Frederik III, Gundestrup, 1995, 39.
7. Maar, 1910, 52-56 and 61.
8. Kircher, 1654, III, 428. The plate is a later addition, not to be found in all copies of the work. The copy used here is: Bodleian Library, University of Oxford. Douce K 141-43. The connection to Kircher and the collection of van Werle is mentioned in a letter from the keeper of the Kunstkammer, J.C. Spengler in 1794, but does not occur in any later Danish sources. Letter dated September 27, 1794. The Royal Library. NKS 1585, 2⁰. I wish to thank Bente Gundestrup for drawing my attention to the let-

ter. Andreasen og Ascani 2013, III, 477-479 (letter nr. 640).
9. Marjorie Caygill of the British Museum has kindly provided me with information on the mummy.
10. Musée de Grenoble. Wooden coffin, 322-31 BC. Donated by J-B de Mure in 1775.
11. Inventory 1690,1. Unpublished. The National Museum of Denmark.
12. Laverentzen, 1710, 1.
13. The coffin, however, is not fashioned after Isis's image but, on the contrary, in the likeness of her spouse, Osiris, a funerary deity, who was a symbol for the rebirth that the Egyptians aspired to attain.
14. I wish to express my gratitude to Helle Salskov Roberts, for assistance on the Latin text.
15. Kircher, 1676, 9-19. Thévenot, 1665, 240-256, *Des Piramides* and 256-262, *Des Momies*.
16. Inv. no. AAa4. Gundestrup, 1991-95, 39.
17. Laverentzen, 1710, 2-3.
18. The catalogue was published for the first time in 1666. Here, the reference is drawn from the 2nd edition of 1674. Olearius, 1674, 72-75, Tab. XXXVI.
19. On the use of mummies for medicinal purposes, see Dannenfeldt, 1985 and Germer, 1995. Bernschneider-Reif, 2007 og Pommerening, 2007. A number of Danish examples are found in Hauberg, 1929, 4-8.
20. Olearius, 1674, 72.
21. Serpico, 2000, 464-468.

22. In Hauberg, 1929, 5 and 6, two preparations are cited from Danish sources. Their constituent ingredients include *mumia of dried human flesh* from *The Land of India* and from a criminal.
23. Germer, 1995, 21-23.
24. Maar, 1910, 149.
25. *Beskrivelse over De Ægyptiske, Græske og Romerske Oldsager i det Kongelige Kunstmuseum* April 1826, inv. no. AAa2. Archives of the Collection of Classical and Near Eastern Antiquities.
26. The doctor, A.B. Granville, who examined an Egyptian mummy in 1821, wrote a rather extensive dissertation. In this paper, there is also an historical survey of a number of mummy examinations. Granville, 1825.
27. Brünnich, 1783. The Kunstkammer mummy and the mummy examined by Brünnich have subsequently come to be conflated, erroneously. See Valdemar Schmidt, 1919, 258, nos. 1517-1518.
28. Brünnich, 1783, 328-329.
29. The remains of the mummy are delineated as no. 5 among the *Ægyptiske Menniske=Mumier*. Brünnich 1782, 8.
30. The Royal Art Museum was a short-lived institution, created for purposes of containing the Kunstkammer's collections of antiquities, art objects and ethnographica, and was the immediate predecessor of the National Museum.

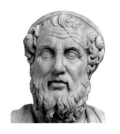

King Frederik V's Acquisitions of Ancient Sculpture for the Royal Academy of Fine Arts in Copenhagen[1]

Mette Moltesen

FOUR ANCIENT MARBLE PORTRAITS

It is not very often that one discovers – or rediscovers – ancient Graeco-Roman works of art in Denmark. In 1989, however, an opportunity presented itself to the Ny Carlsberg Glyptotek: the chance to acquire ten ancient sculptures from a collection of antiquities housed in a Danish country manor, about which no classical archaeologist seems to have previously known.[2] Of course, there may be Greek works, and there are most certainly Roman works, in Danish private collections of which we are unaware. What is even more remarkable is that there are also ancient works of art in public collections which have led lives of obscurity. And this is the case with the marble busts that will be examined in the following. They have indeed undergone a most mercurial existence within the Danish museum system, insofar as their fate has been to wander through a fair number collections entirely dependant on whatever value was accorded them at any one time.

What we have before us are a Socrates portrait that deviates just a bit from the ordinary types, a herm portrait of Homer, a small bearded portrait of a curly-haired Roman, and a portrait of the Empress Livia.

SOCRATES

In an article concerning the portraits of Socrates, which the then director of the Ny Carlsberg Glyptotek, Flemming Johansen, published in 1994 and titled *Socrates in Copenhagen,* he featured an image of a portrait of Socrates which had up to that time spent a considerable portion of its existence tucked away in the basement of the National Museum of Denmark, fig. 1.[3]

Already at the beginning of the twentieth century, in his copy of Kekulé von Stradonitz's *Die Bildnisse des Sokrates,* the founder of the Ny Carlsberg Glyptotek, Carl Jacobsen, had marked this head in red and scrawled the word *Fake!*[4] And in 1962, Helga v. Heintze had crossed off this work from the list of Socrates portraits as an *anerkannte Fälschung.*[5] In more recent times, it has been acquitted of such charges and re-installed and restored to a status of honour and dignity in the gallery of Classical and Near Eastern and Classical Antiquities in the National Museum of Denmark.

Fig. 1.
Marble portrait of Socrates, National Museum
of Denmark, inv.no. ABb 253. Photo Ole
Haupt 1992.

The portrait depicts Socrates with a large, angular skull, in much the same way, in fact, as is often seen in portraits of Plato, with longish curls around the crown of the head and with a most dapper beard, which in a very peculiar way appears to have been combed from out and inwards, towards a reversed parting down the middle in a rather stylized manner. A similar way of representing the beard can be seen, however, on other Socrates portraits of the so-called B-type, among them a portrait in the Hermitage in St. Petersburg and a head in the Capitoline Museum in Rome.[6] The very tightly-packed facial features are distinctive. The head has been carved in Parian marble and measures 37 cm in height and the rounded neck section suggests that the bust was once inserted into the cavity of a mantle-clad statue.[7] The nose is missing but was once restored. At the back of the head there is a cutting measuring 6 × 6 cm which may have served for a clamp to fasten the figure to a wall. In more recent times, the head has been cleaned with acid, presumably to rid the sculpture of calcite accumulations, resulting in a soapy surface. That the head is not unique is substantiated by the fact that another example of the same type was sold at a Sotheby's auction in 1991.[8] It has been suggested that the head could have been made during late Antiquity, in the 3rd or perhaps even the 4th century, AD.[9] It was precisely during this period that portraits of the ancient philosophers, such as Socrates and Plato, enjoyed a renaissance, along with the dissemination of the Neo-Platonic philosophy.

HOMER

In 1999 the Ny Carlsberg Glyptotek presented an exhibition centred on the works of Homer in Denmark, in concert with the reading of Otto Steen Due's new Danish translation of *The Iliad*.[10] In this context, it seemed natural to exhibit all the Homer portraits that could be found in Denmark. The Glyptotek itself owns Roman copies of two of the three known types: the Apollonius type from circa 300 BC., fig. 2[11] and the Hellenistic "Blind Homer" from circa 200 BC,[12] while the early Epimenides type could be represented only by a plaster cast of a head in Munich, which was lent to the exhibition by the Royal Cast Collection, Statens Museum for Kunst, The National Gallery of Denmark.[13]

While working on the preparation of the exhibition, we were alerted to the existence of a Homer portrait which had turned up when clearing the loft of the Christiansborg Palace Church at the end of the nineteen-sixties. Following a small *detour,* it was returned to the nation's collections in 1973, more explicitly, to the Department of Paintings and Sculpture at Statens Museum for Kunst, fig. 3.[14] In his catalogue of older foreign art, compiled in 1980, Harald Olsen had included the head, which appears beneath the caption: *Italy, 17ᵗʰ century (?).*[15]

The portrait is mounted on a bust rendered as wearing a *himation* with vertical folds, on the right side of which the drapery has been hewn away in order to make room for the inscription ΩΜΗΡΟΣ. There are plaster restorations in the beard and the hair and an attached piece — the left side of the forehead and the hair — in marble as well as a new marble nose. In all likelihood, the face has also

Fig. 2.
Marble portrait of Homer,
Ny Carlsberg Glyptotek,
Copenhagen I.N. 609,
Photo Ole Haupt.

Fig. 3.
Marble portrait of Ho-
mer, Statens Museum
for Kunst, Copenhagen,
Department of Paintings
and Sculpture, Inv. 5626.
Photo Ole Haupt.

been very vigorously cleaned of patina and it seems plausible that the wrinkles and furrows around the nose have been touched up. The general impression, however, is that the head is basically antique, whereas the herm bust is a restoration from a more recent date.

The hair, which is shoulder length at the back and bushy at the temples, the thick fillet around the head, the long and curly beard and eyes that seem to be anything but blind, characterize the portrait as belonging to the so-called Apollonius type of Homer.[16] The type is known by this nomenclature because another interpretation had suggested that the portrait could be a representation of the neo-Pythagorean philosopher, Apollonius of Tyana.[17] The identification of the Apollonius type as representing Homer has been widely discussed among specialists and a consensus on this point is yet to be achieved.

This Homer type was already identified by Francesco de Ficoroni (1664-1747) in 1730, when he compared three busts in Cardinal Albani's collection in Rome with Roman coins from Amastris in Paphlagonia, a colony of Smyrna, which had a portrait on the obverse with the inscription, ΩΜΗΡΟΣ. Ficoroni also observed similarities to a drawing of a statuette in the possession of Fulvio Orsini (1529-1600) and mentioned by him in a publication from 1570.[18] This statuette, however, is now lost and only one of the three busts from the Albani Collection appears to be extant: Today it is to be found in the Capitoline Museum.[19]

As our herm bust bears the inscription, ΩΜΗΡΟΣ, we may presume that it was created after the type was identified. Another possibility, of course, is that the inscription is secondary: it might be that the mantle was hewn free at the bottom and the inscription was added only at a later date. As we will see, our head could very well be one of the earliest known examples. It may, in fact, be one of the missing Albani herms. At the same time, the sculptor who restored the hair cannot have been familiar with the Apollonius type, since this type is normally characterised by the fact that the locks of hair over the forehead are all made to face in the same direction and not as here, where the restored locks point every which way.[20]

From the caption in Harald Olsen's catalogue, it appears that the Homer bust was included in the collection of Statens Museum for Kunst in 1908, along with three other heads that also came from the National Museum's Collection of Near Eastern and Classical Antiquities.[21] In 1851, together with the Socrates the bust had made its way from the Royal Academy of Fine Arts to what was known at the time as Antik-cabinettet (the Royal Cabinet of Antiquities), whereas the two remaining heads had already been included in 1825 before the antiquities were set aside as a separate department in 1826.[22]

But while the Socrates bust was regarded as ancient Roman at the time and remained in the possession of the Collection of Near Eastern and Classical Antiquities, the prevailing opinion was that the two other heads (Homer and the

Small Head of a Roman) were modern and should accordingly be placed in the Royal Art Gallery, Statens Museum for Kunst. As we have seen, at a later point in time, a shroud of doubt was also cast around the authenticity of the unfortunate Socrates and he was banished to the basement.

THE SMALL HEAD OF A ROMAN, "MARCUS AURELIUS"

Let us turn our attention to one of the two remaining heads. We have before us a small man's head, mounted on a flat base, fig. 4.[23] It measures only 29.5 cm and depicts a man with a short beard and a curly shock of hair, which is rendered with numerous small short grooves made by a drill, whereas the beard has not been drilled at all. The man turns his head on a disproportionately long neck sharply to his left. The eyes have drilled bean-shaped pupils, and the irises are rendered by incision. The brow is furrowed and the expression is distinctly one of glowering; the mouth is small, with bulging lips. The head has been well preserved and bears traces of an artificial(?) patina. At first glance, one would be tempted to assert that the sculpture represents a Roman emperor from the 2nd century AD, and in the relevant literature, the piece has either been named Marcus Aurelius (AD 161-180) or Septimius Severus (AD 193-211). In Harald Olsen's catalogue, it is listed quite simply as *A Roman*, and described as a 17th century pastiche of a Roman from around AD 200. It is evident that the head is supposed

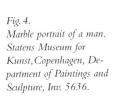

Fig. 4.
Marble portrait of a man. Statens Museum for Kunst, Copenhagen, Department of Paintings and Sculpture, Inv. 5636.

Fig. 5.
Marble portrait of the emperor Marcus Aurelius, Ny Carlsberg Glyptotek, Copenhagen, I.N. 1538, Photo Ole Haupt.

to be a likeness of the emperor, Marcus Aurelius. He was, in fact, depicted with a similar short beard and the thick and spongy crop of hair rendered by numerous drilled grooves. However, the expression on his face is always mild, with somewhat large, kindly eyes, fig. 5. The only Roman emperor who could conceivably be depicted glowering, as we see here, with his head sharply turned, is Caracalla (AD 198-217).[24]

The head is *not* antique. The drilling of the curls has not been fully understood, the small drilled grooves are utilised in a decorative way while failing to follow the hair's natural curls.[25] Nor do the glowering gaze and the long neck appear to be antique. As a matter of fact, the man depicted here rather calls to mind a Prussian officer. When this head was created is another question, on which a more detailed investigation could presumably shed light.

Fig. 6.
Marble portrait of a man, Ny Carlsberg Glyptotek, Copenhagen, I.N. 580, Photo Ole Haupt.

In the study collection of the Ny Carlsberg Glyptotek there is a marble portrait of a bearded man, who on a number of points resembles our small head: the curly hair and the short beard, the small sulking mouth, the brusque expression with the wrinkled eyebrows and forehead, fig. 6.[26] The head was acquired in 1892 and was entered into the inventory as a Hellenistic portrait. Vagn Poulsen (1909-1970), however, regarded the work as being a modern copy of a Lysippean athlete and Flemming Johansen agrees that it is a modern forgery. We find that the Glyptotek's bearded man is certainly modern but this does not automatically mean that the portrait was created as a forgery. In any case, the piece has much in common with our small head.

As has been mentioned, the four heads have not always accompanied one another. In 1825, the Director of the Royal Art Cabinet, Lord High Steward Adam Hauch (1755-1838), informed The Royal Academy that: "a small head in marble, which has been enumerated on the list of inventory as a bust of Septimius Severus, has been declared by the Academy as being suitable for being housed inside the Royal Art Museum."[27] This means to say that the piece had been handed over to the Royal Art Museum, housed at the time in Dronningens Tværgade in Copenhagen. Here, it was entered in the register with the inventory number ABb 20[28] – this figure is inscribed in a highly conspicuous manner on the front of the neck, fig. 4.[29] Later the head was also moved into the Cabinet of Antiquities upon its foundation in 1851.

LIVIA

The fourth head in the ensemble depicts the Empress Livia (58 BC– AD 29), the formidable wife of the Emperor Augustus.[30] It is a most beautiful portrait of an apparently youthful woman. According to the old inventory of the Cabinet of Antiquities, the head was once mounted on a large draped bust, fig. 7: "In addition, there is a veil that hangs down over both shoulders. Arms and breasts were covered with a thin, albeit folded flowing robe. On the right arm, there are 4 buttons, on the left there are 3, by means of which this garment was fastened together from the shoulders on down. The head is looking slightly downward. On the face, the nose and especially the lower part of the cheeks have been restored [sic!]. There are no pupils in the eyes. The head is mounted on a pedestal of marbled wood and is purported to be the bust of Queen Berenike or Cleopatra or the Empress Agrippina." On a photograph from one of the rooms in the National Museum's Collection of Near Eastern and Classical Antiquities taken sometime around 1931, we can see the large Livia bust on display, fig. 8. In a later photograph from 1938

Fig. 7.
Digitalized reconstruction of the portrait of Livia as it was restored in the 17th century, Thora Fisker.

Fig. 8.
Portrait of Livia as exhibited in the National Museum of Denmark c. 1931.

it appears that the portrait has been removed from the veiled bust and the neck is mounted directly on a low base. The portrait, however, still has its restored diadem and part of the cloak intact, fig. 9.[31]

The Livia portrait was dealt with for the first time by Walter Gross in 1964 in his article on the portraits of Augustus and Livia in the National Museum in Copenhagen.[32] By that time, the bust had long since been removed and moreover, the crown of the head with the diadem had also been taken off, leaving the head cut off just above the forehead. The horizontal attachment surface is antique and reveals that the portrait, also in antiquity, had the upper part of the head made in a separate piece of marble, fig. 10. The remaining fragment of white, fine-grained marble (probably from Carrara) measures 27.5 cm and the head is therefore larger than life. Gross considered the head one of the very finest portraits of Livia, belonging to the so-called Salus type.[33] This portrait type was created in the last years of the empress's life and used extensively after her deification in AD 41. It is found in two representations in the portrait gallery of the Ny Carlsberg Glyptotek. One is a colossal head from the theatre at Cerveteri in Etruria, fig. 11[34] and the other a large, handsome statue found in a Roman villa at Pozzuoli in Campania where the empress is represented carrying a cornucopia.[35] The head from Cerveteri also had the upper part with the diadem attached as a separate piece of marble.[36] This is a very common technique in sculpture of the first century AD.

In her monograph on the portraits of Livia, Elisabeth Bartman argues that the head, rather than being a depiction of Livia herself, is in fact a portrait of the

Fig. 9.
Marble portrait of the empress Livia, National Museum of Denmark, inv. no. ABb 2, removed from the bust and mounted on a low base ca. 1938.

Fig. 10.
Marble portrait of the empress Livia, National Museum of Denmark inv. no. ABb 2 after removal of the crown of the head and the diadem c. 1964.

Fig. 11.
Marble portrait of the empress Livia, Ny Carlsberg Glyptotek I.N. 1422. Photo: Ole Haupt.

Fig. 12.
Draped bust of the baroque period originally mounted with the portrait of the empress Livia, National Museum of Denmark, inv.no. ABb 2. Photo: Ole Haupt.

Emperor Caligula's favourite sister, Drusilla, represented in a manner that intentionally bears a similarity to that of her great-grandmother, Livia.[37] And one thing that Livia and Drusilla certainly had in common was that they were both deified after their deaths. If, however, we compare the portrait from Cerveteri with our Livia, they appear to resemble each other so closely that they can only be said to depict one and the same person.[38]

It is clearly obvious that the large and voluminously draped bust was a restoration.[39] This marble bust has for many years been stored away under the rafters of the National Museum, fig. 12. After cleaning its appearance is that of a magnificent piece of baroque marble sculpture probably the work one of the many artists working in the restoration business in Rome in the 17th and 18th century.

The reason why the portrait bust could have been taken to be a representation of the Egyptian Queen Berenice can be traced back to the gold coins from Ephesos upon which Queen Berenice II (272-221 BC) is seen in profile.[40] Here, she is indeed sporting a similar coiffure, replete with diadem and a mantle over her head. Other Egyptian queens were depicted in much the same manner; this is also true of Cleopatra. That the portrait was ever identified as Agrippina (AD 15-59), the wife of the Emperor Claudius, or Faustina (AD 105-141), the wife of the Emperor Antoninus Pius, is harder to fathom, since they were both represented with completely different kinds of coiffure.

THE ANTIQUITIES IN THE ROYAL DANISH ACADEMY OF FINE ARTS

On February 15, 1825 a letter from Lord High Steward Adam Wilhelm Hauch was put before the Royal Academy of Fine Arts with instructions to exchange the Academy's marble bust of Agrippina (i.e. our Livia) for the Royal Art Museum's plaster casts of the Capitoline Venus and nine heads of Roman emperors.[41] The proposal was complied with and together with the small head of the Roman man, fig. 4, the Livia portrait was transferred to the Royal Art Museum and assigned the number ABb 2 in the inventory of works of ancient art. All of the four marble heads that have been treated here, then, have once belonged to the Royal Academy of Fine Arts.[42]

The Royal Danish Academy of Fine Arts was created in 1754 and was thus much younger than the academies in France (1665), Vienna (1692), Stockholm (1735) but a little older than the academy in St. Petersburg (1757). There had been smaller academies, giving lessons in drawing and painting but it was only in 1754 that the king, Frederik V (1723-1766), donated his private palace, Charlottenborg, to be the seat of the Royal Academy.

On October 3rd, 1754 the four heads were officially handed over by Carl Gustav Pilo (1711-1793) to the collection of the newly established Royal Academy of Fine Arts.[43] Pilo was a professor of painting at the Academy as well as the Court Painter to King Frederik V. For this reason, he had an official residence in the palace where the Academy was housed, and the marble heads had been placed in his keeeping.

However, one could already have seen the portraits on exhibition the previous year since the sculptures for the grand hall at Charlottenborg had already been moved there by November 1753.[44] Just how they were arranged was noted in *Kjøbenhavnske Danske Post-Tidender* no. 99, published on December 10, 1753, which mentions the re-location of the Royal Academy from the side wing of Christiansborg Palace to Charlottenborg Palace.[45] "In the large hall for the assembly of the directors and professors, wherein for the use of the Academy is placed:

at the entrance, on the left-hand side. 1. **A Head of Marble, called Homer,** on the right-hand facing the town square 2. the Grecian Venus, at whose right side stands Faunus, and an antique head, and on the left side stands Apollo and the head of a Vestal Virgin. 3. an antique figure, the original of which is found in the gallery in Florence. 4. An anatomical horse and on the right side, two heads, **Marcus Aurelius made of marble** and an Apollo made of plaster". What follows is a series of plaster casts, among these being the Laokoon group from the Vatican, "10. **a bust portrait of Berenice,** and 11. at the exit on the left-hand side, a **Head of Socrates in Marble;** moreover, around the perimeter of the hall, busts of the 12 first emperors."[46]

Following a detailed report of how King Frederik's consort, Queen Juliane Marie (1729-1796), had made a promenade to Charlottenborg and then back again, one could already have read, on March 30 1753 in the *Post-Tidender* no. 26, that: "for purposes of its [i.e. the Academy's] use and benefit, His Royal Majesty had imported from Italy 4 antique marble statues, which have been entrusted to Professor Pilo, while the Academy's move to Charlottenborg Palace is underway."

It appears to be something of an exaggeration that mention is made here of *statues.* But the article gives us the valuable information that the sculptures had been acquired from Italy. As we shall see, however, they had not come directly from there, but by a considerable detour. The article also tells us that the antique statuary in the academy, in much the same manner as the plaster casts of renowned masterpieces, were intended to be used as models for the art students.

KING FREDERIK V'S ANTIQUITIES

The donor was, thus, King Frederik V, who was not otherwise known for being a great collector, at least not of antiquities.[47] In 1791, a small catalogue was published, treating the: "MARBLE and PLASTER FIGURES, as well as THE RECEPTION-PIECES and a number of WORKS OF ART in the Royal Academy of Painting, Sculpture and Architecture at Charlottenborg with appended concise statements clarifying some of the most important entries."[48] From this list, it becomes evident just how important our four heads were thought to be, as a matter of fact, they constituted the entire section on marble works in the catalogue. In the large Sculpture Hall the pieces are actually mentioned as: "Genuine Antiquities in Marble No. 1. A Bust. Some are of the opinion that this bust is a portrait of Faustina, the consort of the Emperor Antoninus Pius, others, on the other hand, advocate that the head must be Berenice, a daughter of Agrippa, King of Judea.[49] Thereupon Heads: 2. Socrates 3. Homer 4. Septimius Severus." Subsequently the plaster casts are enumerated, the Apollo Belvedere and Laokoon and his sons, etcetera.

It is worth noting that only the female portrait is named as a bust, while the other three portraits are listed as heads. This could have been an indication that the head of Homer was first set into its herm *after* having arrived at the Academy. The small head of a Roman emperor is now called Septimius Severus rather than Marcus Aurelius.

A more internationally oriented Copenhagener could, however, have read in the French-language *Mercure Danois* of April 1753, under the heading, *Beaux-Arts*, that, at Charlottenborg, one would presently be able to see: "quatre Bustes antiques dont le Roi a tout nouvellement fait l'acquisition; Savoir les Têtes de Socrate, de Marc-Aurelle, de Platon & de Bérénice. Celle de Socrate, est jugée être d'une grande antiquité & toutes sont d'une beauté parfaite" – and now comes the important part – "Ces Pièces sont tirées du Cabinet du feu Prince Eugène de Savoye."[50] The fact that the newspaper confuses Homer with Plato adds further substance to the supposition that, at the time, the head had still not been provided with its inscribed bust but could also merely be a lapse.

Apparently not everybody agreed on the exceptional quality of the heads, this is apparent from a comment made by Friedrich Wilhelm Basilius von Ramdohr (1757-1822), who, in his book on his impressions from a visit to Denmark, provides a detailed account of the Royal Academy of Fine Arts in 1792. He mentions the Socrates head, calling it a poor work, whereas the Roman woman with diadem (Livia), is a fine piece of sculpture, whereas the other two heads are not mentioned at all.[51]

PRINCE EUGENE OF SAVOY'S COLLECTION OF ANTIQUITIES[52]

It thus appears that King Frederik V had purchased the four marble heads from the collection of the late Prince Eugene of Savoy, an exceptional collection put together by a truly remarkable man.[53]

Eugene was the fifth son of Prince Eugene-Moritz of Savoy and Soissons (1635-1673), and lived from 1663 until 1736, fig. 13. He was born in Paris where his mother Olympia Mancini (1640-1708), a niece of the great cardinal Mazarin, was part of the French court and a childhood sweetheart of King Louis XIV.[54] Because of his fragile health Eugene was originally intended for the priesthood and indeed obtained the lowest grade in the Catholic Church, that of abbé. Instead, he came to be one of the greatest military commanders of his day, indeed of all time. When, as a young man, he sought to serve in the military in France, King Louis XIV would not accept him in spite of his French background. Dressed as a girl he fled France and enlisted in the active service of the Habsburg Emperor Leopold I (1640-1705) in Vienna. Already in 1683 Eugene made a name for himself in a battle against the Turks whose siege of Vienna had penetrated as far as the

outlying districts of the city itself. In 1697, he was entrusted with overall command of the Austrian army and fought valiantly at Zenta, thus expelling the Turks from Hungary.[55] In the War of the Spanish Succession (1701-1714), Eugene was governor general of Milan and had command of the Imperial forces in Italy.[56] In alliance with the English he also fought battles against the French in the Netherlands alongside the other great general of the time, his brother in arms, the Duke of Marlborough (1650-1722).[57] For his valour in battle Queen Anne of England (1665-1714) gave him a diamond studded sword. As a matter of fact, Eugene fought on just about every battlefield in Europe. He modelled himself on his great hero, the Roman emperor Marcus Aurelius (AD 161-180), who combined the life of a soldier with that of a stoic philosopher. There were many similarities between the two, Marcus had also been considered weakly as a child, and like Eugene he fought the barbarians, the Marcomanni, to protect Vienna on the Eastern borders of the Roman Empire, and finally like Eugene he died in Vienna. No wonder that Eugene owned a portrait thought to represent this emperor.

In between military campaigns, which meant every winter, Eugene lived in Vienna as a patron of the arts and a great building entrepreneur. He constructed a grand *palais* inside the city and on the outskirts he built the magnificent Belvedere Castle with J.L. von Hildebrandt (1668-1745) as architect. He also amassed a large collection of works of art, consisting especially of Dutch and Italian old master paintings.[58] Eugene was an ardent reader and his library was ordered systematically and scientifically in a more modern fashion than was normal in the baroque period. His *Bibliotheca Eugeneia* of c.15.000 volumes was bought by the emperor in 1737 and came to form the nucleus of the National Library in Vienna and his large collection of prints is now in the Albertina Museum.[59]

Since Eugene died a bachelor and left no immediate successors, it befell his niece, Princess Anna Victoria of Savoy (1683-1763), to sell off the objects in his collections following his death.[60] "With an excessive covetousness that was truly nauseating, she simply tried, and as quickly as possible, to convert everything her uncle had left her into cash".[61] Eugene's vast collection of paintings was acquired by Duke Charles Emmanuel III of Savoy in Turin, and was later brought to Paris by Napoleon. The greater part is now housed in the Galleria Sabauda in Turin.[62]

It does not appear, however, that Prince Eugene was particularly interested in antiquities nor did he possess an extensive collection. The few antiquities that he did possess can rather be considered diplomatic gifts, but several of them have come to acquire a great deal of significance in classical art history.

THE HERCULANEUM WOMEN

The most magnificent sculptures in Prince Eugene's collection were the three female statues that became known as the Herculaneum Women. The statues had been found in 1709/10 during the first excavations in Portici, which eventually led to the discovery of the ancient Roman city of Herculaneum which had been covered in lava by the eruption of Vesuvius in AD 79.[63] Here, the statues had probably decorated the *scenae frons* of the Roman theatre. They were discovered in the grounds of a country house that belonged to Emanuel Moritz of Lothringen, Prince d'Elboeuf (1677-1763), who was the general commanding the Imperial troops in Naples. It was he who in 1713 made a present of the statues to Eugene, as a diplomatic gift.

The three statues represent two types of female statues the originals of which were the work of Greek artists in the late 4th century BC and became immensely popular in the Roman period when they were used as models for for portraits of Roman elite women.[64] The large Herculaneum Woman, an over-life sized representation of a woman draped in a large cloak also covering the head, was used for older women whereas the Small Herculaneum Woman was used primarily for younger women. The three name-giving statues in Eugene's possession were one of the Large Herculaneum type and two of the Small Herculaneum type, one with its head preserved and one without.

The three statues served as the central elements in the layout of the so-called Marble Gallery in The Lower Belvedere, which became Eugene's summer residence in 1714, fig. 14.[65] The back wall in this gallery had five niches. In the middle one was placed the statue of the Large Herculaneum Woman, and in the outer niches on the right and on the left, there were the statues of The Small Herculaneum Woman, and a torso of the same type, which was restored with a copy of the head of the former. Among these works, there were baroque statues representing Apollo, Adonis, Diana and Ariadne created by Domenico Parodi (1668-1740), an Italian painter and sculptor who worked for the prince.[66] The

Fig. 14.
The Herculaneum Women in the Marble Gallery of the Lower Belvedere palace reproduced by Salomon Kleiner 1740, from Aurenhammer 1969, pl. 99.

aa. *Renards des Indes.*
b. *Chamois.*
c. *Belier de Walachie.*
d. *Chat Sauvage.*
e. *Loup des Indes.*
f. *Grand Perroquet.*
g. *Belier Tripolitain.*

Sal. Kleiner. I. E. M. del.

h. *Civette.*
i. *Antique de marbre blanc.*
k. *Arbre a poix Resine.*
l. *Sedum Africanum folio et viridi luteo variegato.*
m. *Tithymaloïdes Africana, non latescens Squamato caule Simplica.*

Cum Pr. Sac. Cæs. Maj.

aa. *Indianische Füchse.*
b. *Gambs.*
c. *Wallachisch Schaaf.*
d. *Wilde Kaß.*
e. *Indianischer Wolff.*
f. *Indianischer Rab.*
g. *Wilder Wider von Tripoli.*

Hæred. Ier. Wolff. exc. Aug. V.

h. *Indianische Kaße.*
i. *Antique Statue von weißen Marmor.*
k. *Winder-Baum oder rother Dannen sive Picinus.*
l. *Sedu Africanii folio et viridi luteo variegato.*
m. *Tithymaloides Africana non latescens Squammato caule Simplici.*

Iacob Gottlob Thelott Sculps.

three ancient statues represented the "edle Einfalt und stille Grösse" of Winckelmann in contrast to the vigorous movement of the baroque sculptures.

The Belvedere Castle in Vienna was illustrated by Salomon Kleiner (1700-1761) in a series of copperplates showing Vienna in the baroque period. In Volume X, from 1741, that is to say four years after Eugene's death, Kleiner depicts the statues as they had been exhibited as decorative elements in the representation of Eugene's *Menagerie,* fig. 15 and when they later stood in the marble gallery.[67] After the death of Prince Eugene, they were acquired by Elector Friedrich August II of Saxony (1733-1763) (King August III of Poland) and were brought to his capital, Dresden, where they still are regarded as some of the most eminent masterpieces of the collection of ancient sculpture.[68]

While here they were mentioned in enthusiastic figures of speech by Johan

Fig. 15.
The Small Herculaneum Woman among wild animals in Prince Eugene's Managerie, reproduced by Salomon Kleiner, from Aurenhammer 1969, pl. 105.

Joachim Winckelmann (1717-1768), who described them, paying particular attention to the folds of their garments, in his very first work on antique statues, *Gedanken über die Nachahmung der griechischen Werke in der Malerei und Bildhauerkunst* (1755), which he authored in Dresden before ever having been to Italy himself. He regarded the statues as representing vestal virgins, whereas they were probably rather portraits of women from Herculaneum, and praised them for the way in which the drapery was rendered in lively folds emphasising the body beneath. This he regarded as a characteristic of the finest ancient Greek art. That Eugene also regarded these statues as exceptional works of art is clearly apparent from the fact that he changed the plan of the marble gallery to incorporate them as the main focus of attention. In his book, Winckelmann says of Eugene: "Dieser grosse Kenner der Künste, um einen vorzüglichen Ort zu haben, wo dieselben konnten aufgestellt werden, hat vornehmlich für diese drei Figuren einen Sala terrena bauen lassen, wo sie nebst einigen anderen Statuen ihren Platz bekommen haben."[69] He informs us, moreover, that all of Vienna had been thrown into a state of commotion when the statues were sold and carried off to Dresden.

THE PRAYING BOY

Another treasure from Prince Eugene's collection is the bronze statue of *The Praying Boy,* now in the Antikensammlung in Berlin.[70] It was allegedly unearthed on the island of Rhodes and was brought to Venice already in 1503. Since that time, it had been in a sequence of important collections in Verona and Mantua, even later passing into the possession of King Charles 1 of England. The French minister Nicolas Fouquet (1615-1680) had the statue restored supplying it with new arms and placed it in his palace at Vaux-le-Vicomte. In 1717 his son sold it to Prince Eugene for 18.000 Francs. Following Eugene's death, the statue came into the possession of another great general, Joseph Wenzel of Lichtenstein (1696-1772) who subsequently sold it to King Friedrich II "Frederick the Great" of Prussia (1712-1786), who displayed it in his palace, Sanssouci. In 1806, *The Praying Boy* came to Paris, as part of Napoleon's war booty but was returned to Sanssouci after the fall of Napoleon in 1814. From 1830 it has been exhibited in the Antikensammlung in Berlin.[71] Modern studies have given rise to the supposition that the statue was cast on Rhodes around 300 BC by a sculptor who had studied with the famous Greek sculptor Lysippus.[72]

One utterly unparalleled work of art in Prince Eugene's library was the road map of the Roman Empire copied in the 13th century, which we know as the *Tabula Peutingeriana*.[73] It was named after the antiquarian Conrad Peutinger (1465-1547) of Augsburg, who owned the map around 1500. After Eugene's death, it was purchased – along with the remaining contents of his library – by

Emperor Charles VI (1685-1740) for the library in Vienna, where it can still be seen today.

So we can certainly say that the collection from which the Danish king purchased his works of ancient art was a prestigious one. There are not many ancient sculptures in the Danish public ownership that descend from Central European princely collections. Nevertheless it would be interesting to see whether it is possible to trace the busts still further back in time. Unfortunately, there are no proper catalogues or lists of Prince Eugene's sculpture collection and the only well-known ancient sculptures in the Belvedere Castle seem to have been the three Herculaneum Women. Despite all good intentions, it has until now not been possible to identify the few other sculptures that appear in the engravings of Eugene's Belvedere.

THREE ROMAN CARDINALS

Fortunately, in *Partikulærkammeret*, a special royal household account for the use of the Danish monarchs, entries can be found covering the acquisition of the four busts in 1752.[74] It appears that the four portraits were purchased through the Danish envoy in Vienna, Johann Friedrich Bachoff v. Echt (1710-1781) at a price of 490 two rix-dollars, a considerable sum of money. In an *addendum* to the balance sheet, the four heads are enumerated and described:

"1. La Berenice suivant l'estampe ci-iointe [the print is now missing]
2. Une magnifique tête d'Homere avec son buste de la Hauteur de 2. pieds environ.
3. Une tête de Socrate avec la buste â peu près de la meme hauteur. Cette Tête est de Phydias le premier et plus ancien sculpteur de la Grèce.
4. Une tête inconnue.

Ces statues sont toutes Greques du bon tems et très bien conservées. C'est tout ce que feu le Prince Eugène avvis en bustes antiques. Il les a lües de Rome des Cardinaux Albani, Passionei, et Colona. Ces pièces servient d'ornement à sa Bibliotheque."[75]

This virtually amounts to a sales pitch, wherein all four heads are transformed into Greek masterpieces. The head of Socrates is brazenly touted as nothing less than a creation of Phidias himself. We also learn that the Homer portrait, in fact, already had its inscribed bust and that the Socrates head was also placed in a bust of similar size.

The entry also shows that the heads were the only ancient busts that Eugene possessed and that they were placed in his library. Eugene's main library was in

Fig. 16.
The library of Prince
Eugene in the Upper Bel-
vedere Castle, reproduced
by Salomon Kleiner, from
Aurenhammer 1969,
pl. 18.

his winter palace in the centre of Vienna, but he also had a library in the Belvedere. In S. Kleiner's publication there is an engraving of Eugene's library in the Upper Belvedere with three book-cases on which busts are placed, fig. 16. These Aurenhammer simply defines as "philosophers", fig. 16.[76] If we look closely on the book-case to the left there stands what seems to be a bald man with a beard on a nude herm which could very well be our Socrates. On the next book-case is a draped herm with a bearded head which, from the shape of the drapery, could be our Homer. On the book-case to the right there is a bust with the head turned sharply to its left which seems to have a curly head of hair, and could therefore very well be our small "Marcus Aurelius". May we surmise that our Livia was placed on a book-case at the other end of the room?

Thus we have been able to identify some further works of ancient art from Eugene's collection.

It is interesting to have the confirmation that the route of acquisition of the heads leads back to Italy, as Eugene had acquired them from the collections of the Roman cardinals Albani, Passionei and Colonna.

Cardinal Alessandro Albani (1692-1779) was the most prominent collector of antiquities of his day who, during his lifetime, built up no less than two vast collections, the second with the aid of J. J. Winckelmann. This collection is still exhibited in the Villa Albani at Porta Salaria in Rome.[77] For some time, Cardinal Albani served as a papal nuncio in Vienna and during this time concluded a *concordat* with the Kingdom of Savoy (1726). This earned him the protectorate of Savoy, which meant that when he returned to Rome he represented Austrian interests at the papal court.[78]

We know that Alessandro Albani supplied Eugene with paintings so it would not be surprising if he had wished to honour the Prince with a diplomatic gift of a piece of ancient sculpture. In his activity as a collector Albani came into contact with many of the wealthy English travellers in Rome and he became a willing spy for the English, reporting in detail on the plans and plots of the "Old Pretender", James Stuart (1688-1766) and later on those of his son, young Charles Edward Stuart, "Bonnie Prince Charlie".[79] Albani reported when James was gathering troops, so the English were ready when he landed in Scotland in 1745.

However, it could also have been his elder brother, Cardinal Annibale Albani (1682-1751), who was supplying Eugene with antiquities. Alessandro and Annibale were nephews of the Albani pope, Clement XI (1649-1721) and some of the most influential persons in Rome at the time. Annibale was also a collector, especially of books, coins and artworks, most of which have by now been transferred to the Vatican collections. For a certain period, Annibale Albani was the diplomatic representative of the Saxon prince-elector in Rome, and from 1719 until 1747, he was *cardinal camerlengo* of the Holy Roman Church. This implies that he was responsible for issuing permits to carry out excavations in the Papal States. He supplied Eugene with many fine books for his library and, in a engraving, we can see a copiously decorated study, where the cardinal is instructing Prince Eugene, fig. 17.[80] Accordingly, it could very likely be either one of the two Albani cardinals who also supplied Eugene with one or more of the four heads. Furthermore, it seems plausible that one of these might very well have been the Homer portrait, since we have already observed that there were at some time three examples of the Apollonius type of Homer in the Albani Collection and that there is allegedly only one now remaining there (see p.32).

Cardinal Domenico Silvio Passionei (1682-1761) had been Archbishop of

Ephesus in Asia Minor, where he could very well have acquired some ancient sculptures. Later on, he was papal nuncio in Vienna and one of Eugene's closest friends who provided him with information about manuscripts and books from Italy.[81] Later still, in 1755, he became cardinal librarian of the Vatican library. His funeral sermon for Eugene was published in 1737 and distributed all over Europe. In it he said that in Eugene were combined the spark of Hannibal, the resolution and activity of Caesar and the virtue of Trajan.[82] He might very well also have made Eugene a gift of an antique portrait – although we cannot guess which one this could have been.

The Colonna family possessed the magnificent palace at S. Apostoli in Rome. Here, the very finest sculpture gallery that was known in that day was established. In the 17th century large-scale excavations in the Duchy of Marino along the Via Appia on the way to the Alban Hills had supplied the Colonna family with many pieces of ancient sculpture.[83] Here, in the area of ancient Bovillae (modern Fratocchie) several ancient Roman villas were excavated and numerous famous sculptures were unearthed.[84] In the following century, the Colonna collection was enlarged by the addition of other collections through marriage into other Roman aristocratic families. It certainly seems reasonable to assume that Cardinal Girolamo Colonna Di Sciarra (1708-1763), Eugene's contemporary, could have supplied him with a fine Roman portrait. The *gens Iulia* was worshipped in Bovillae, so a fine head of Livia, adopted by Augustus' will into the Julian family as Julia Augusta, would not be out of place in that area.[85] In the Colonna collection, there are several portraits of Roman emperors from the 16th and 17th century, one of a young Marcus Aurelius in particular, a small "modern" head of a Roman would also have been a possible gift.[86]

In his book on the Upper Belvedere Peter Stephan interprets Eugene's self representation as a prince and warrior in the artistic adornment of his palace as a manifestation of himself as the man without family who lays down his life and soul in the service of the Austrian emperor whom he regarded as a kind of foster father. Instead of a gallery of ancestor portraits, as was common among the aristocracy, Eugene draws on his spiritual ancestors, heroes from mythology and history: Hercules and Alexander, Aeneas and Scipio, Perseus, Theseus and Jason.[87] The same could be said of the representations in his library in the Upper Belvedere. Here Eugene wishes to demonstrate his life as a scholar and art lover represented, as we have seen, by the busts of Homer, Socrates and "Marcus Aurelius" and supported by the representations over the door frames of personifications of "Jurisprudence", to the left "Poetry" and "Theology" to the right. A stucco emblem over the fireplace represents the triumph of science, and below it there is a statuette of the Spinario.[88] This antique figure of a young boy was widely copied in bronze in the 16th and 17th centuries and often used as a diplomatic gift to royalty. The painting over the fireplace shows Diana, Goddess of the Hunt, and the stucco reliefs in the corners of the ceiling, Diana and Endymion, Juno and Leto, while the painting in the centre of the ceiling depicts Leto with her children Apollo, the protector of art and science, and Diana deity of animals and nature. All the motifs come from ancient mythology and fit well with Eugene as the creator of a large menagerie with rare plants and animals, and as the owner of a library containing books on science and art. In this room strife and battle are absent and Eugene could forget the battlefields and feel like a scholar and collector.

CONCLUSION

Three Roman portraits and a small curly-haired head from the seventeenth or eighteenth century made their way from Italy via Vienna to Copenhagen where they comprised the entire collection of marble works at the Royal Danish Academy of Fine Arts from 1753 to 1825, as far as two of the heads are concerned, and up to the year 1851, when it comes to the two others. After that time, they were part of The Royal Art Museum and later on of the Cabinet of Antiquities. In 1908, both Homer and the "Marcus Aurelius" were handed back to The Royal Art Museum, now the Statens Museum for Kunst, because they had come to be regarded as modern works, while Livia and Socrates remained in what was now the Collection of Near Eastern and Classical Antiquities in the National Museum of Denmark as ancient Roman works. Then, Socrates was relegated to the cellar as a modern piece – and there remained but one, namely the stately bust of the empress Livia. Subsequently Socrates has been re-assigned to antiquity and now Homer has also been blessed with the same resuscitation – so now we have three! Now, fortunately, the heads are again united in the National Museum.[89]

Scheibler, I. 2004
Rezeptionsphasen des jüngeren
Sokratesporträts in der Kaiserzeit,
JdI 119, 179-258.

Stephan, P. 2010
Das obere Belvedere in Wien,
Architektonisches Konzept und
Ikonographie. Das Schloss des
Prinzen Eugen als Abbild seines
Selbstverständnisses, Wien.

Verschüttet vom Vesuv 2005
Die letzten Stunden von
Herculaneum, J. Mühlenbrock &
D. Richter red.

Vierneisel Schlörb, B. 1979
Glyptothek München, Katalog
der Skulpturen Band II, Klassische
Skulpturen, München.

Winckelmann, J.J. 1755 (Reclam
1995) Gedanken über die
Nachahmung der griechischen
Werke in der Malerei und
Bildhauerkunst, Berlin.

Winkes, R. 1995
Livia Octavia Julia Porträts und
Darstellungen. Louvain-la-Neuve.

Zimmer, G. and Hackländer, N.
eds. 1997
Der betende Knabe, Original und
Experiment,
Antikensammlung Staatliche
Museen zu Berlin Preussischer
Kulturbesitz, Berlin.

Zimmermann, K. 1977
Die Dresdener Antiken und
Winckelmann, Berlin.

Notes

1. The article builds on a lecture similarly entitled, from the seminar, *Denmark and Antiquity in the 1700s,* under the network: The Role of the Artist in the Rediscovery of Antiquity, May 11-12 2000. I am grateful to curators Bodil Bundgaard Rasmussen and John Lund for their willingness to incorporate the article in the present volume and for permission to publish the two heads in the Department of Near Eastern and Classical Antiquities in the National Museum of Denmark and to the late museum curator Olaf Køster for permission to publish the two heads in the Statens Museum for Kunst.

2. Ny Carlsberg Glyptotek I.N. 3688-3693; H.I.N. 923-924; Æ.I.N. 1792-1793. *Medkøb* 46, 1990: J. Christiansen, "En klassiker", pp.5-24; M. Moltesen, "En romersk vognstyrer", pp.25-45; F. Johansen, "Hvem er den tykke mand?", pp.46-58.

3. The National Museum's Collection of Near Eastern and Classical Antiquities ABb 253; Johansen, 1994, 48 fig.17.

4. Kekulé 1908, 50, no.9.

5. v. Heintze, in: Hekler 1962, 54 note 16; Richter 1965), 115, no.9. Here Richter refers to a letter from V. Poulsen which states that the head had already been removed from exhibition.

6. Richter 1965, figs. 505-507; Hermitage Museum, St. Petersburg IN 2348; Scheibler, 2004, 197-198, fig.10; Richter 1965, 112 no.6, figs.487-489.

7. The marble analysis was made by Professor Norman Herz, University of Georgia, Athens Georgia.

8. Sotheby's, London 8.7. 1991, no.288; Johansen 1994, 48 fig.18.

9. The head has, however, not been included in Scheibler 2004.

10. *The Iliad–Book and Image,* Ny Carlsberg Glyptotek, Copenhagen 1999.

11. NCG Cat., Greek Portraits 1992, no.47, I.N. 609.

12. NCG Cat., Greek Portraits 1992, no.59, I.N. 2818.

13. The Royal Cast Collection, Statens Museum for Kunst, Inv. KAS 2237, plaster cast of a portrait in the Glyptothek, Munich Inv. 273; Vierneisel Schlörb 1979, 36-48;

14. Nørbæk 1972, 8, note 3, mentions that the bust had been entrusted to the care of the Christiansborg palace administration shortly after having been transferred to the Statens Museum for Kunst in 1908.

15. Inv. 5626. II, 97. Olsen 1980, 69.

16. Richter 1965, 48-50; an overview of the research on the Apollonius type can be found in Böhringer & E.Böhringer 1939, 42-54.

17. Richter 1965, 49, 284.

18. Böhringer & Böhringer 1939, 44, pl.17.

19. Musei Capitolini Inv. 591, Helbig, I⁴ no.1359; Böringer & Böhringer 1939, 59-60, Replik III, pl.23 below.

20. Richter 1965, p.49.

21. Here the head had been inventoried with the number ABb 252.

22. Hermansen 1951, 9-56.

23. Statens Museum for Kunst Inv. 5636. II, 101. Olsen 1980, 69-70.

24. For example, Ny Carlsberg Glyptotek I.N.2028, NCGCat. Roman Portraits III, 36, no.9.

25. In the middle of the back of the head, there is a small dowel socket, the purpose of which cannot readily be explained.

26. Ny Carlsberg Glyptotek I.N. 580; NCGCat.,Greek Portraits,154 no.64.

27. Quoted from a copybook in the Royal Academy of Art: 20. December to Hauch.

28. In the register, the classical archaeological specimens are listed with an A, and the ABb designation covers "Monuments of stone and fired clay, statues, busts, anaglyphs, inscriptions, etc."; Hermansen 1951, 49.

29. In a copy of Pilo's deed of conveyance of 1754 in the Department of Near-Eastern and Classical Antiquities, however, it has been identified with a portrait of Marcus Aurelius ABb 1, by a marginal note made in P.J. Riis's hand. This portrait is, however, made of bronze and placed in a monumental marble bust.

30. Department of Near Eastern and Classical Antiquities ABb 2; Winkes 1995, 122-123, fig.45; Lund & Rasmussen 1995, 158-162, fig.159; Here the head has been re-mounted on an old, profiled, red marble base.

31. Negative D 273 from the Department of Antiquities; Gross1964, 53 fig.2.

32. Gross, 52-60.

33. Named after coins representing Livia as Salus Augusta from 22 AD; "Der Typ mit Mittelscheitelfrisur" (Salus type) Winkes 1995, 44-50; Bartman 1999, 112, fig.6.

34. NCGCat., Roman Portraits I 1994, 100-101, no.38 from Cerveteri; Winkes 1995, 120 no.44; Bartmann 1999, 154, cat.17, figs. 100-101. From the reign of Claudius (AD 41-51).

35. NCGCat., Roman Portraits, 102-103, no.39 from Pozzuoli; Winkes 1995, 119-129, no.43; Bartmann 1999, 158, cat.28, figs.105-106. From the period of Claudius (AD 41-51); *Augusto* 2013, 205, cat.III,5.

36. Winkes 1995, 122-123 shows the two heads together.

37. Bartman 1999, 221, no.5; pp.126-127. From the time of Caligula (AD 37-41).

38. Winkes op. cit.; Bartman op.cit., 126-127, figs. 99-100 evince great similarities with one another.

39. In the old register it reads: *Height: 1 alen* [ca. 2 feet] *and 5 inches; Width across the breast and from arm to arm: slightly in excess of 1 alen* [ca. 2 feet].

40. Kraay 1966, colour plate 20, no.804, pl.219, no.802.

41. Meldahl & Johansen 1904, 512; The Capitoline Aphrodite, Lange1866, 48, no.109. It has not been possible to identify the portraits in the inventory of the Royal Cast Collection.

42. I would like to express my warmest thanks to Emma Salling, former librarian at the Royal Danish Academy of Fine Arts, for many interesting items of

information about the heads, which I have permitted myself the luxury of citing. They were found in The Danish National Archives in connection with her work on the history of the Royal Academy of Fine Arts, Fuchs & Salling 2004.

43. Cf. *Partikulærkammeret*, addendum to the accounts 1748-30/9 1767. Entered on the balance sheet as No.23, folder 31/8 1752 1/1 1754.

44. Meldahl and Johansen 1904, 39.

45. Quoted in Mehldal and Johansen op.cit., 40-41.

46. Saabye 1973), 20, note 37. The twelve emperors are now exhibited in the anteroom to the National Museum's Collection of Near Eastern and Classical Antiquities. Bundgaard Rasmussen, 2000), 141-157.

47. Hein 1996, 245-266.

48. *FORTEGNELSE over MARMOR OG GIBSFIGURERNE, samt RECEPTIONSSTYKKERNE og FLERE KONSTSAGER i det kongelige MALER-BILLEDHUGGER- og BYGNINGS-ACADEMIE paa CHARLOTTENBORG med HOSFÖYET KORT FORKLARING over DE BETYDELIGSTE POSTER*, Kiöbenhavn 1791, 2.

49. This is another Berenice, born in 28 AD, the daughter of King Herod Julius Agrippa of Judea, renowned for living together with her brother, Agrippa II, and for having a long-lasting affair with the future emperor Titus.

50. Ramdohr 1792, 164.

51. *Four antique busts, which the king has recently purchased: this means to say, heads of Socrates, Marcus Aurelius, Plato and Berenike. That of Socrates is considered to be very old*

and all of them are very beautiful. These pieces come from the cabinet of the late Prince Eugene of Savoy.

52. I am grateful to museum curator A. Bernhard-Walcher at the Kunsthistorische Museum in Vienna for providing many interesting references to Prince Eugene's collections.

53. Prince Eugene 2010, 24-29.

54. Rumour even had it that Louis XIV might have been Eugene's natural father.

55. I. Ortayli in: Prince Eugene 2010, 49-73.

56. Prince Eugene 2010, 80-95.

57. Prince Eugene 2010, 97-102.

58. C. Diekamp in: Prince Eugene 2010, 127-153.

59. G. Mauthe in: Prince Eugene 2010, 191-223.

60. Eugene was known to be a homosexual and among his fellow officers was called "Mars without Venus".

61. Noll 1963, 59.

62. Per una storia del collezionismo sabaudo 1982; C.E.Spantigati in: Prince Eugen 2010, 275-283.

63. Verschüttet vom Vesuv 2005, 274.

64. Daehner 2007; Knoll & Vorster 2013, 170-183, cats. 33-35.

65. Noll 1963; Krapf & Krapf 1993, 15 ff; Gschwantler 2000, 159.

66. Prince Eugene 2010, 162-163, cat. III. 27.

67. Aurenhammer 1969, 106, pl. 99; Prince Eugene 2010, 163, cat. III. 24.

68. Noll 1963, 59-63; Knoll 1993, 30-31, nos. 13 and 14; Daehner 2008, 73-91, 101-127; Knoll &Vorster 2013, 170-183, cat. nos. 33-35. The ancient sculpture collection in Dresden is at the present time (2014) not on view but will be reopened in the Semper Gallery in 2017.

69. Winckelmann 1755 (1995), 17-20; Protzmann 1977, 33-44.

70. Antikensammlung Berlin Inv. SK 2; Die Antikensammlung 2007, 63-64, No.31 Kabus-Preisshofen 1988, 679 ff. Gschwantler 2000, 160; Prince Eugene 2010, 160, cat. III.23.

71. A bronze copy of The Praying Boy belonged to the founder of the Ny Carlsberg Glyptotek Carl Jacobsen and is now on show at the Carlsberg Academy in the outskirts of Copenhagen.

72. Zimmer & N. Hackländer1997; Andreae 2001, 59-60, cat. I.2.

73. Bosio 1983 passim; Mraz 1985, 263; Prince Eugene 2010, 110, cat. II.96.

74. *Partikulærkammeret*, list of accounts for 1752 Fol. 180-181; no.1175 Dec. 9, 1752 with addendum. Emma Salling has kindly referred me to this document.

75. *1. Berenike, as the enclosed engraving, 2. A magnificent head of Homer, with a bust measuring almost 2 feet in height, 3. A head of Socrates with a bust having almost the same height. This head was made by Phidias, the first and oldest sculptor in Greece. 4. An unidentified head. These statues are all Greek, from the finest period, and they are very well preserved. This comprises the total of what the departed Prince Eugene had in the way of antique busts. He had leased (acquired?) them from Rome, from the cardinals Albani, Passionaei and Colonna. These pieces served as the artistic adornment of his library.*

76. Aurenhammer 1969, 44, pl.18; Prince Eugene 2010, 206, cat. IV.13.

77. Röttgen 1982, 123-152.

78. Röttgen op. cit., 141; Prince Eugene 2010, 200- 201, cat. IV.5.

79. Lewis 1961, 124-129.

80. Prinz Eugen und das barocke Österreich 1986, 129, 4.28; Prince Eugene 2010, 200, cat. IV.2; engraving in Budapest, Magyar Nemzeti Muzeum Inv. 4280.

81. Mraz 1985, 242; Prince Eugene 2010, 290, cat.VI.11; Cardinal Passionei in an etching by Nicolò Billy the Elder in the Austrian National Library in Vienna.

82. Prince Eugene 2010, 291, cat. VI.12.

83. Galleria Colonna 1990,18-34.

84. De Rossi 1979.

85. Bartman 1999, 114.

86. Galleria Colonna 1990, 213-14, no.115.

87. Stephan 2010, 190-198.

88. Haskell & Penny 1988, 308-310.

89. The National Gallery of Denmark has given the portrait of Homer and the little head of a Roman as a long term loan to the National Museum.

The Unacknowledged Consul: Carl Christian Holck as Collector of Antiquities in Tunisia, 1801-1807[1]

John Lund

In 1807 the Danish Prince Frederik – who was later to become King Frederik VI – set up the so-called Royal Commission for the Preservation of Antiquities. Time had run out on the honourable Kunstkammer, and it was accordingly the commission's task to indicate "how, with a minimum degree of expense to the nation, a state museum could be established".[2] Thus the seeds were sown for the National Museum. One of the leading commission members, the extremely knowledgable Frederik Münter, wrote to the egyptologist and antiquarian Georg Zoëga in Rome that it was not only going to be "the Nordic, but just as much the Roman and Greek [antiquities], which were going to be displayed in this museum".[3]

With this in mind, it is not surprising that the Commission was entrusted with some fragments of marble sculptures from North Africa on December 30, 1810, along with the following letter: "During my sojourn in Tunisia I have found, in the ruins of Uttica, a marble head, two feet and one hand, all of an extraordinary size. And is an honour for me to forward these ancient relics to the Commission for the Preservation of Antiquities, with the intention that they be included in the collection of the Royal Museum. With the utmost respect, Holck".[4]

The donation must have attracted some measure of interest, seeing that only a few fragments of ancient statues had managed to find their way to Denmark by the beginning of the nineteenth century.[5] Nevertheless, these sculptural fragments and their donator, Carl Christian Holck (1758-1816), were consigned to oblivion – notwithstanding the fact that they, together, inaugurate one of the most exciting chapters in the formative history of the Collection of Classical and Near Eastern Antiquities: a tale of how the eighteenth century's North African pirates were indirectly responsible for the National Museum's acquisition of a distinguished collection of antiquities of Roman date from Tunisia.

Fig. 1.
Fragment of a mosaic in The
Collection of Classical and
Near Eastern Antiquities, i.n.
ABb 107.

THE FINDS FROM *UTICA*

The Commission passed the sculptures from Utica on to The Art Museum in Dronningens Tværgade in Copenhagen, and in 1833 the protocol of this museum informs us that seven "ancient marble fragments, found in Tunisia, have been received from the Royal Commission for the Preservation of Nordic Relics". Inside the Art Museum, they were grouped together with the antiquities from the now-defunct Kunstkammer in "the collection of classic antiquities from the southern territories" also known as the Cabinet of Antiquities"[6] – one of the forerunners of the National Museum's present Collection of Classical and Near Eastern Antiquities.

The enumeration of no less than *seven* received antique pieces comes as a surprise: Holck, as we have seen, mentions only four fragments. The most obvious explanation, perhaps, is that he had subsequently handed over three additional finds to the Commission. No matter how this story can be pieced together, two of the three extra objects, "a piece of an arm",[7] and "a piece of a leg",[8] were lost many years ago.

As far as the third additional find – "a fragment of a mosaic floor" – is concerned, the story, fortunately enough, works out in a clearer way, fig. 1.[9] And as

Fig. 2.
Marble fragment of a statue: a hand holding a spear, i.n. ABb 103.

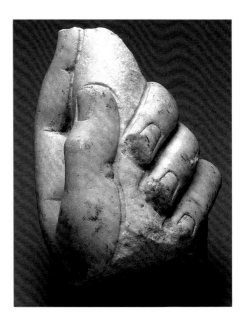

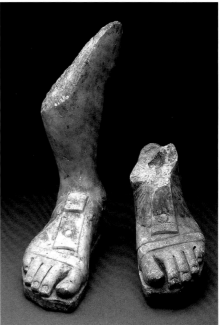

Fig. 3.
Marble fragments of a statue: two feet, i.n. ABb 105-106.

much can be said of the fragments that were mentioned in the original deed of gift: a left hand, grasping a staff – ostensibly a spear, fig. 2,[10] and two sandal-clad feet, fig. 3.[11] For obvious reasons, we cannot say very much about how the sculptures in question actually appeared, and it is far from certain that the hand originates from the same statue as do the feet. The same goes for the last of the finds, which can in all probability be identified with a larger-than-life size head of a young man with sideburns, figs. 4–5. On the basis of its style, this fragment may be dated to Roman Imperial period, more precisely to the second half of the 2nd century AD.[12]

AN ENIGMATIC PORTRAIT

Upon closer examination, the head reveals itself to be a portrait of Alexander the Great, who died in 323 BC after having subjugated a great part of the Greek world and of the Middle East. The identification is corroborated by the ram's horns protruding back around both ears, since Alexander was the only mortal who was depicted with this peculiar ornamentation of the head. The horns refer to the Egyptian sun god, Ammon, who had the ram as his sacred animal. The Greeks identified Ammon with Zeus, and when Alexander after his conquest of Egypt in 332 BC paid a visit to Zeus Ammon's oracle sanctuary at the Siwa oasis, the priests greeted him as the god's son.[13]

Figs. 4-5.
Fragment of a marble statue: a portrait of Alexander the Great, i.n. ABb 97.

Fig. 6.
Silver tetradrachms, struck
in or shortly after 321
BC by Ptolemaios I,
after Breitenstein 1941,
figs. 3-4.

The back of the head and the neck of the portrait bust are covered by an elephant's scalp, and just over the forehead, what can be seen is where the animal's trunk and tusks originally protruded. This unusual headdress presumably refers to Alexander's conquest of India.[14] He was not portrayed in this manner during his lifetime, but on silver tetra-drachms coined in or about 321 BC under Ptolemaios I,[15] who became king of Egypt after Alexander's death, fig. 6, the great conqueror is decorated with an elephant's scalp and ram's horns, a combination that was probably intended to lead the mind toward Egypt and India, two of the outer geographic limits of Alexander's empire.[16] The head from Utica is most likely a Roman copy of a contemporary portrait of Alexander.

In 1941, Niels Breitenstein published the Alexander portrait and persuasively expounded its art historical significance. But he was hardly correct in identifying the piece with "the alabaster head of a cherub with gilded wings", which Christian Tuxen Falbe, the Danish consular general in Tunisia from 1821 until 1832, brought back to Copenhagen.[17] What speaks against this supposition is that a "cherub" – or cupid – is usually depicted as a plumb winged boy who is seldom if ever depicted in larger-than-life size. For this reason alone, the identification is implausible. Moreover, the Alexander head is not supplied with gilded wings, and its sideburns substantiate that we are not dealing with a child here.[18] On top of all this, the well-traveled Falbe, who was interested in geology, could not possibly have conflated the portrait's large-grained marble with alabaster – a white, Egyptian type of stone. And being an expert numismatist, he supposedly would have proceeded to quickly trace the true identity of the portrayed person.[19]

DENMARK AND THE MEDITERRANEAN IN THE EIGHTEENTH CENTURY

But who was Carl Christian Holck, and how did he manage to come into possession of the antiquities in question? In order to answer these questions, it is necessary to move back in time to the eighteenth century, when Denmark was an autocratically-governed regional super-power, the realm of which extended from Norway's northern tip to Schleswig-Holstein and subsumed Greenland, Iceland and the Faroe Islands as well as overseas colonies. Denmark was an agricultural nation with hardly any industry to speak of, which nonetheless – thanks to a cautious policy of neutrality – reaped the benefits of an almost uninterrupted period of peace lasting from 1720 to 1807. During this period, the Danish merchant marine, one of the largest in Europe, fetched home great profits.[20]

In order to protect the merchant marine's ships, it was necessary for Denmark to maintain a powerful navy. Something of the kind was for instance required in the Mediterranean region, one of the important areas for Danish seafaring.[21] The fact was that the so-called Barbary states of North Africa, Morocco, Algeria,

Tunisia and Tripolis (present-day Libya) had been thriving ever since the 17th century on ambushing trading ships and taking possession of their crews as slaves. This took place within the context of privateering – a not uncommon practice in those days, which implied that private ships could obtain a state license to ambush enemy merchant ships in return for part of the booty. The North African corsairs were not restricted to the Mediterranean Sea. As a matter of fact, they attacked Iceland in 1627 and kidnapped 242 inhabitants, and they took thirty women as captives a few decades later on the Faroe Islands. Consequently, there were Danes among the Christian slaves in North Africa who were living with a (not entirely unrealistic) hope of being ransomed one day.[22]

The leading trading nations Denmark among them – were of the opinion, whether right or wrong, that it would be difficult and expensive to restrain and quell the pirates. Instead of trying to do so, they decided to sign treaties with the Barbary states, which stipulated that every year, 'protection money' would be paid in the form of precious gifts to the local princes, who would return this consideration by refraining from attacking the agreeing partners' ships.[23] A diplomatic presence became necessary hereafter in order to ensure that the signed agreements were being complied with.[24]

HOLCK ENTERS THE SCENE

On October 31, 1801 a newly-appointed Danish consul stepped ashore in Tunis. This man was 43-year old Carl Christian Holck, fig. 7,[25] who – as was the custom – was accompanied by his wife, 25-year old Henriette, fig. 8.[26] Trudging along just behind them were their 5-year old son, Martin Ludvig Georg Ferdinand, and a Danish maid and a servant.

Holck had made a name for himself in the navy, where as a Captain, he had distinguished himself at a sea battle off the coast of the Libyan capital of Tripoli in 1796 – a skirmish from which the small Danish naval unit was extraordinarily lucky to escape.[27] The crew on the brig, Sarpen, praised him in a song penned shortly after the sea battle: "Our chief, he is such a brave fellow, and Christian Holk is his name. God grant him happiness and honour, to promote his and our welfare. May God hold his hand over us, then we will strike boldly for king and country. We have forced the Turkish dog to make eternal peace with Denmark, since in his own home he found the Dane to be fearless. And now our ships are free of the restraints and slavery of the Turk".[28]

Holck's superior officer, Steen Bille, was most satisfied. He declared that Holck deserved "to be decorated for the fine order and businesslike procedure that existed on his ship ... his unremitting and evident enthusiasm and eagerness in the face of duty, when he was ordered to go forth on any expedition, were always the same – and unflagging in his service, he had continually proved ... all

Fig. 7.
Miniature portrait of Carl Christian Holck, probably painted by Friederich Carl Grøger in the summer of 1808.

Fig. 8.
Miniature portrait of Henriette Holck, likewise presumably painted by Friederich Carl Grøger in 1808.

of which taken together causes me to state that I have had a great deal of delight in having him under my command".[29]

OFFICIAL DUTIES

As it came to pass, Holck's period of residence in Tunis lasted until 1807. We can follow the course of his family's life, in fine detail, from one day to the next, through a perusal of his scrupulously written diaries and accounts.[30] For example, one can read about his somewhat tense relationship with the country's regent, Sidi Hammuda Bey, who was living inside the Bardo Palace – presently serving as Tunisia's National Museum. Holck characterized him as "a prince with a great deal of natural ingenuity, but his shortcoming is an extreme degree of greediness, etc".[31] The diary gives a number of examples of the regent's petty-mindedness.

On February 2, 1805, for example, Holck was "at the Bardo in the company of the Bey, who told me in the company of the Minister, Sidi Jussuff: 1) that he was not pleased with the watch and the chain studded with diamonds, 2) with the diamond ring, which was a solitaire ring, the Bey was pleased, 3) the Bey does like the cloth, but wanted me to compensate him for the lengths that were missing, 4) the yards were missing, but there were several ship's beams that were two inches thinner but somewhat longer than the other beams – to carve the yards from, 5) I got the Bey to give up his request for 100 barrels of tar and 100 barrels of pitch along with the two barrels of tar which had leaked out during the voyage. Sappa Tappa was indeed pleased with the cannons and the gun-carriages; the Bey also likes them and will make gun-carriages for larger cannons of this shape. – [I] was lucky that the Bey dropped his request for the sacks of chewing tobacco … Now nothing of what was wanted and what was promised is missing … except for the rifles and pistols inlaid with gold, the brocade and the Attagan trimmed with diamonds".[32]

The yatagan mentioned here is a Turkish weapon: a kind of curved sword, which was worn hanging from the belt. In the ensuing five years, a considerable part of the correspondence between the Danish consulate in Tunis and the Royal African Consulate-Direction in Copenhagen is concerned with this very expensive ornamental weapon, the appearance of which is known from a drawing presently in the National Record Office.[33] Holck did his utmost to get the Bey to withdraw his request for the yatagan, but without any luck. The consul did manage, however, to delay the transfer of this valuable item until the year 1811.

SORROWS AND DELIGHTS

The diary delineates a living portrait of a country were snakes and scorpions, illness and famine were almost part and parcel of everyday life. For example, on March 30, 1805, Holck noted that "People are dying of hunger in the streets in Tunis; they are eating grass and soil".[34] And again, on March 6, 1806: "A Moor [dead]… of hunger just outside our house". Four days later, he writes that "everyday, the Bedouins are fighting over bread".[35]

The more prosperous part of the population, to which the European minority belonged, evidently had no problems obtaining food. But to a great extent, they were smitten with the same widespread diseases as the rest of the local population, especially a plague-like "putrefaction fever". A diary entry made in the spring of 1806 recounts an "endless extent of disease; the Moors are lying spread out on the street in this rain; these are the people who have moved in from the countryside – they have nothing and even if they could pay, there is simply no room for them. The gates of the city are lying full of Moors. When one has to ride out through the city gate, it is difficult to move through the passage without becoming nauseated by a horrible stench".[36]

But life there was also filled with a number of bright spots – especially the time spent together with other Western emissaries and their families.[37] The consulates

Daignés agréir, Madame, Co Joibble Ouvrage

avec L'assurance de mon Since et hommage
Charles Tulin

Fig. 9.
Water colour painted by
Clark Charles Tulin to the
Album Amicorum of Hen-
riette Holck.

were situated in the city of Tunis. But during the warmer summer months, the diplomats moved about 15 kilometers outside of town to La Marsa – a pastoral area with gardens situated not far from the coast. It is quite possibly the Holck family's country home which can be seen in a watercolour painted by the Swedish consul, Clark Charles Tulin, fig. 9. This work was glued into Henriette Holck's "album amicorum", inside of which friends and acquainttances signed their names alongside a verse or a drawing, in much the style of the signature albums of later times. Charles Tulin also painted a second watercolour in the album: a landscape with palm and cypress trees and a view out over a bay looking toward three characteristic mountains, fig. 11.

MEETINGS WITH ANTIQUITY

From La Marsa, the Europeans made excursions to the ruins of nearby Carthage, which had once been the center of the Western Phoenician – the so-called Punic – culture, until the Romans eradicated the city from the face of the earth

An humble attempt by & meant to express the respectful *regard* for *you* of Madam your very devoted little friend
Alexandre Tulin

Fig. 10.
Water colour painted by Alexandre Tulin to the Album Amicorum of Henriette Holck.

in 146 BC.[38] However, Carthage was resurrected from the rubble of its own ruins during the reign of Augustus Caesar and the city gained importance once again – now as the capital of a Roman province. A watercolour in Henriette Holck's album which is signed "your devoted little friend Alexandre Tulin" depicts a lagoon-like lake with a few characteristic mountains in the background, fig. 10 – a motif which very well might have been inspired by ancient Carthage's naval harbour.[39] Holck writes about the ancient city: "You see only … some ruins, a few cellars and a few cisterns; but you can still get a sense of what kind of power Carthage must have possessed, sitting there beside the ruins of the superb aquaduct which exists for an extent of 'ten [Danish] miles' [=ca. 46.8 miles], which once conveyed spring water into Carthage … Spread out everywhere through the whole kingdom, you see the ancient relics of Tunisia, or rather the ruins, inasmuch as there are very few remarkable remnants – and these continue to erode every day".[40]

On September 24, 1804, Holck ate "lunch with my family near the cisterns

Fig. 11.
Water colour painted by
Clark Charles Tulin to the
Album Amicorum of Hen-
riette Holck.

at Carthage ..." and "took a whole Carthage stone home with me. It is a mosaic and a base of a temple". And according to the diary, he was with his "family at Carthage" on April 3, 1806, at which time he "obtained an ancient base, which was deposited into a box". Aside from the mosaic, which is probably the piece presently in possession of the Collection of Classical and Near Eastern Antiquities, fig. 1, these finds cannot be identified today. The same thing can be said of most of the medals, coins and "antiquities" that Holck acquired whenever the opportunity presented itself – as it did, for example, on March 31, 1805. On the very same day, he paid the jeweler, Pottier, 14 [Tunisian piasters] "for [setting] a ring",[41] which is supposedly identical with a silver finger ring that Professor I. Holck sold to the Collection of Classical and Near Eastern Antiquities in 1867 together with four ancient "gems" – a designation for seals made from semi-precious stones, figs. 12-13. These were brought home to Denmark by Carl Christian Holck and "were presumed to originate ... from the excavations at the ruins at Utica that were being carried out at the time".[42]

The most interesting of these is a scarab of cornelian with a depiction of a sitting dog, which has been carved "in negative" into the stone; the motive is figured out in such a way that it will be seen as a positive imprint.[43] This scarab has been perceived as being Etruscan, but it was not only in Egypt – and later in Etruria – that seals were fabricated in the form of scarabs, and what we have here may rather be Punic scarab from the 5th–4th century BC, which should not come as any surprise seeing that Utica was one of the oldest and most important cities in the Punic world.[44] The other gems are Roman – with perhaps the exception of the cornelian with a depiction of a sitting Hercules, which could very well be a "modern" forgery.[45] On one of the other gems, there is a standing woman holding a branch and a spike in her hands.[46] And on the third, a child under a tree can be seen.[47] On the stone set into the ring, there is a sword, two greaves, a breastplate, a spear, a shield and at the top, a helmet with a feather-plume.[48]

HENRIETTE HOLCK

It might have been the case that it was most especially Henriette Holck who was interested in these gems.[49] In any event, she addressed an inquiry to the most knowledgeable antiquarian at the place – a Dutch lieutenant going by the name of Jean Emile Humbert – in order to obtain an expert opinion about some of the pieces.[50] His respose, however, was rather insipid: "… What you wanted, madam, is an explanation about the ring you are wearing around your finger, but I am in possession of too little knowledge about such antiques to be able to flatter myself with having satisfied your request. But the most learned men in such matters would say, as do I, that your little gem's greatest value must be attributed to the hand that wears it".[51]

In 1804, on approximately half of the year's days, Holck noted: "My wife is

Figs. 12-13.
Gem stones brought to Denmark by Holck, which were sold by an heir to the National Museum in 1867, i.n. 110-114.

not well" or "My wife is sick"; he writes about obtaining medicinal remedies and that sort of thing. But nothing seemed to help.[52] Henriette's condition hardly improved upon her reading of a long poem about the angel of friend-ship which the consulate's secretary, Henrik Vilhelm Lundbye,[53] wrote in her album on December 29, 1805: "Soon, my very special female friend, you will be leaving us, and it will be a bitter moment of farewell for all of us who have come to understand your heart, your spirit and who have been worthy of your noble friendship. – For me, who sees your exquisite conduct, who enjoys your friendship … Oh, for me, the hour of separation will be painful. But wherever destiny's tidings may lead me, the memory of you will always follow me, and I will continue to bless this keepsake with gratitude!".[54]

As it came to pass, in the following summer the moment of departure was imminent, and Henriette Holck could now travel back to Italy with the couple's two children – in the meantime, they had brought forth another son, Peter Carl Christian.[55] In January 1807, it was Carl Christian Holck's turn to leave the country. But the trip took a dramatic turn when the ship he was on ran aground on sand banks off the coast of the harbour town of Porto Farina in northern Tunisia, where Holck was literally stranded for almost two months while waiting for the ship to be repaired.

EXCURSION TO UTICA

In Porto Farina, Holck was warmly received by the Danish vice-consul, Gaspari, and frequently hosted by the highest ranking local official: the Kaya. But the waiting time dragged on and on, and it was presumably a welcome way of pass-ing the time when on February 3 [1807], he made an excursion to the nearby ruins of Utica.[56] Through a perusal of his diary, we can follow him along the way.

"Travelled to Utica with the Kay[a] of Porto Farino in the company of the Iman, or priest, in Porto Farino, Sidi Assein, and Gasparie in his carriage – along with the Kay[a]'s domestic servants. When we arrived in Utica, an octagon tent was pitched, inside of which we dined … [I] found a pedestal at Utica which had been excavated there, as the Bey is digging for ashlar stones among the ruins. On the pedestal, the following was inscribed: LIBERO PATRI – AVG – SACRUM. There had been a male figure with his long hair hanging down, who was naked. But the Mohammedans, who generally do not like figures, had severed the head, the hands, the feet and the male member, turned the figure on its stomach and thrown the figure – and a dog which stood next to it, into the water. The Kay[a] quickly issued an order to remove the figure from the water, which was complied with as we stood there".[57]

The inscription, fig. 14, tells us that what we had here was a statue of Liber Pater – a Roman counterpart to the Greek god of wine, Dionysus. Liber Pater, as a matter of course, was depicted as a young long-haired man – often accompanied by the wine god's special creature: a panther – possibly the "dog" mentioned in the diary's text.[58] This statue has apparently never been seen later travellers. It has, as likely as not, been lost – or else it is standing unrecognised in some out-of-the-way-place, inside some museum or other, in Tunisia or Europe. The diary is silent about the sculptural fragments, which Holck handed over to the Royal Commission for the Preservation of Antiquities in 1810. But he must have stumbled upon these in connection with this – his first and only – visit to Utica.[59] And thus, in a peculiar way, we have come right back to our starting point. This seems to be the appropriate place to take our leave of Carl Christian and Henriette Holck.[60]

THE ERA OF THE CONSULS

In the larger context, Holck's collection of ancient relics is situated at a crossfield between two epochs. On the one hand, there is a distinct affiliation with the tradition from the time of the Kunstkammer, where antiques were perceived for the most part as matters of curiosity. And in much the way that Moritz Hartmand, upon his return from Athens in 1688, donated the two Parthenon heads to the Danish king, Holck also handed over his most interesting antiques to the nation in 1810.

On the other hand, Holck's activity also points toward what was to come. His observations about the statue at Utica and its inscriptions can – with some measure of goodwill – be regarded as the humble beginnings of a new and more scientific approach to the ancient world. Henriette Holck's appeal to Lieutenant Humbert for the purpose of learning something more about her gems can be interpreted in the same manner. But it is first with the tenure of Holck's successor, Andreas Christian Gierlew (1774-1845),[61] that we can trace a more systematic interest in the country's past – an approach that was brought to its culmination during the tenure of the next Danish general consulate in Tunis, C.T. Falbe (1791-1849, who studied the country's rich ancient legacy in a scientific fashion, carried out excavations and sent hundreds of antiques back to Denmark.[62]

One of the explanations for the prodigious growth of the Collection of Classical and Near Eastern Antiquities' in the nineteenth century is that some of the Danish envoys in the Mediterranean countries regarded it as part of their duty to send ancient relics back to Denmark. Holck was one of the first – but far from the last – to do so.[63]

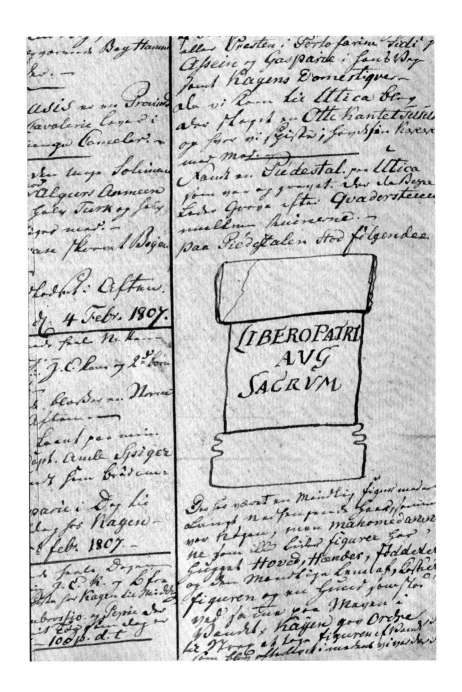

Fig. 14.
A page of Holck's diary with a sketch of the inscription from Utica.

Bibliography

Ahlem, J.B. 1992
Le culte de *Liber Pater* en Afrique a la lumiere de l'épigraphie, in: Mastino, A. (ed.), L'Africa romana. Atti del IX convegno di studio Nuoro, 13-15 dicembre 1991. Sassari, 1049-1065.

Andersen, D. 1995
Farligt møde i Middelhavet, Siden Saxo 12 nr.3, 12-19.

Andersen, D. 1996
Denmark-Norway's Golden Age in the Mediterranean, in: Sørensen, S. og Schiro, J. (eds.), Malta 1796-97. Thorvaldsen's Visit. Based on the unpublished Diary of Peder Pavels. La Valetta, 9-20.

Andersen, D. 2000a
La politique danoise face aux États barbaresques (1600-1845), in: le Bouëdec, G. and Chappé, F. (eds.), Pouvoirs et litoraux de XVe au XXe siécle. Rennes, 243-250.

Andersen, D. 2000b
Søløjtnant Uldall, Pasha Sidi Yussef og lidt om Bertel Thorvaldsen. En nyfunden dagbog fra et middelhavstogt 1796-97, Maritim Kontakt 22, 51-77.

Andersen, N.A. 1966
Nogle politiske Guld-Yataganer fra Algier og Tunis, Vaabenhistoriske Aarbøger 13, 159-226.

Andreasen, Ø. and Ascani, K. 1967-2013
Georg Zoega. Briefe und Dokumente 1-5. Kopenhagen.

Bosworth, A.B. 1977
Alexander and Ammon, in: Kinzl, K.H. (ed.), Greece and the Eastern Mediterranean in Ancient History and Prehistory. Studies Presented to F. Schachermeyr on the Occasion of his Eightieth Birthday. Berlin, 51-75.

Breitenstein, N 1941
To alexandrinske Hoveder in: Arkæologiske og Kunsthistoriske Afhandlinger tilegnede Frederik Poulsen 7.3.1941. København, 87-94.

Ciccotti, V. 1999
Camillo Borgia (1773-1817) soldato ed archeologo, Quaderni della Biblioteca Comunale 8. Velletri.

Ciccotti, V. (udg.) 2000
Atti del convegno internazionale di studi Camillo Borgia (1773-1817), Velletri 18 novembre 1999. Velletri.

Debergh, J. 2000
L'aurore de lárchéologie à Carthage au temps d'Hamouda bey et de Mahmoud bey (1782-1824): Frank, Humbert, Caronni, Gierlew, Borgia, in: Khanoussi, M., Ruggeri, P. and Vismari, C. (eds.), Geografi,

viaggiatori, militari nel Maghreb: alle origini dell'archeologia del Nord Africa, L'Africa romana 13. Roma, 457-474.

Debergh, J. 2005
Jean Emile Humbert et les premières découvertes puniques à Carthage: stèles et inscriptions funéraires et votives, i: Atti del V congresso internazionale di studi fenici e punici, Marsala-Palermo, 2-8 ottobre 2000. Palermo, 293-302.

Feldbæk, O. 1997
Storhandelens tid. Dansk Søfartshistorie. 3. 1720-1814. København.

Fischer-Hansen, T. 1990
Sizilien und Dänemark, Acta Hyperborea. Danish Studies in Classical Archaeology 2, 169-188.

Fischer-Hansen, T. 1997
Frederik Münter og Saverio Landolina. Et venskab, Meddelelser fra Klassisk Arkæologisk Forening 37, 22-33.

Fischer-Hansen, T. 2009
Frederik Münter in Syracuse and Catania in 1786: Antiquarian legislation and connoisseurship in 18th century Sicily, in: Giarrizzo G., Pafumi, S. (eds.) OGGETTI, UOMINI, IDEE. Percorsi multidisciplinary per la storia del

collezionismo: Atti della tavola rotonda Catania, 4 dicembre. – Pisa and Roma, 117-137.

Fredricksmeyer, E.A. 1991
Alexander, Zeus Ammon, and the conquest of Asia, TransactAmPhilAss 121, 199-214.

Gasparri, C. 1986
S.v. Dionysos/Bacchus, in: Lexicon Iconographicum Mythologiae Classicae (LIMC) III 1. Zürich/ München, 540-566.

Grimm, G. 1978
Die Vergöttlichung Alexanders des Grossen in Žgypten und ihre Bedeutung f r den ptolem"ischen Königskult, in: Das ptolemaische Žgypten. Akten des Internationalen Symposions, 27.-29. September 1976 in Berlin. Mainz, 103-109.

Halbertsma, R.B. 1991
Le solitaire des ruines. De archeologische reizen van Jean Emile Humbert (1771-1839) in dienst van het Koninkrijk der Nederlanden. Leiden.

Hansen, A.H. 1999
"Tre smaa Stÿkker, af uvis Bestemmelse …" En Studie i Nationalmuseets ægyptiske Samling 1826-66. Registrering og Genstandsopfattelse. Speciale i Ægyptologi.

Holck, H. 1951
Kommandør Carl Christian Holck og hans Hustru Bolette Henriette Margrethe Lund. Holte.

Holck, H. 1962
Kommandør Carl Christian Holcks dagbøger som konsul i Tunis, Personalhistorisk Tidsskrift 82. Årgang, 14. Række, 4. Bind. København, 61-129.

Holm-Rasmussen, T. 2001
Danskeren Georg Zoëga – arkæolog, numismatiker, ægyptolog og koptolog i Rom, in: Christiansen, E. (ed.), Arven fra Ægypten II. Genopdagelse Mystik og videnskab. Aarhus, 117-122.

Jakobsen, T.B. with assistance from Adamsen, Ch. (eds.) 2007
Nationalmuseets Oprindelse. Oldsagskommissionens Mødeprotokoller 1807-48, Acta Archaeologica 78, 185-334.

Jensen, J. 1992
Thomsens Museum. Historien om Nationalmuseet. København.

Kienast, D. 1987
Alexander, Zeus und Ammon, in: Zu Alexander d.Gr. Festschrift G. Wirth zum 60. Geburtstag am 9.12.86, 1-2. Amsterdam, 309-333.

Krarup, P. 1976
Due archeologi danesi. Georg Zoega e Peter Oluf Bröndsted, in: Mélanges d'histoire ancienne et d'archéologie offerts à Paul Collart. Lausanne, 277-284.

Leclant, J. and Clerc, G. 1981
S.v. Ammon, in: Lexicon Iconographicum Mythologiae Classicae (LIMC) I 1. Zürich/ München, 666-689.

Le Glay, M. 1981
S.v. Africa, in: Lexicon Iconographicum Mythologiae Classicae (LIMC) I 1. Zürich/ München, 250-255.

Lund, J. 1986
The Archaeological Activities of Christian Tuxen Falbe in Carthage in 1838, Cahiers des Études anciennes 18, 8-24.

Lund, J. 1992
C.T. Falbe: Dansk agent og antikvar i Tunesien 1821-1832, in: Grinder-Hansen, K. (ed.), Rejsen. København, 89-101.

Lund, J. 1995
En draperet kvindestatue fra Utica i Nationalmuseets Antiksamling, Klassisk Arkæologiske Studier 2. Copenhagen, 195-214.

Lund, J. 2009a
Royal connoisseur and consular collector: the part played by C.T. Falbe in collecting antiquities from Tunisia, Greece and Paris for Christian VIII, in: Bundgaard Rasmussen, B., Steen Jensen, J. og Lund, J. (eds.), Christian VIII & The National Museum. Copenhagen, 119-149.

Lund, J. 2000b
Il console Gierlew e il conte Borgia in terra d'Africa, in: Ciccotti (ed.), 74-83.

Lund, J. 2000c
Archaeology and Imperialism in the 19th Century: the Case of C.T. Falbe, a Danish Agent and

Antiquarian in French Service, in: Jacquet, P. and Périchon, R. (eds.), Aspects de l'archéologie française Au XIXème siècle, Actes du colloque international tenu à La Diana à Montbrison Les 14 et 15 octobre 1995. Montbrison, 331-350.

Lund, J. 2008
"En viid og rig Mark for Undersøgelser": Danmark og den tidlige arkæologiske udforskning af Tunesien, Nationalmuseets Arbejdsmark, 115-132.

Lund, J. 2014
Tunisia under Danish eyes: The role of Christian Tuxen Falbe and other Danes in the incipient archaeological exploration of Tunisia, in: Mezzolani, A. & Dridi, H. (udg.), Under Western Eyes. Bologne, 33-49.

Marquard, E. 1952
Danske Gesandter og Gesandtskabspersonale indtil 1914. København.

Mørkholm, O. 1991
Early Hellenistic coinage: from the Accession of Alexander to the Peace of Apamea (336-188 B.C.). New York/Port Chester/Melbourne/Sydney.

Redissi, T. 1999
Etude des empreintes de sceaux de Carthage, in: Rakob, F. (ed.), Karthago III: Die deutschen Ausgrabungen in Karthago. Mainz am Rhein, 4-92.

Reinheimer, M. 2001
Der fremde Sohn. Hark Olufs' Wiederkehr aus der Sklaverei. Neumünster.

Richter, G.M.A. 1965
The Portraits of the Greeks III. London.

Rumpf, A. 1963
Ein Kopf im Museum zu Sparta, AM 78, 176-199.

Sauer, H. 1964
Das Motiv nachalexandrinischer Köpfe mit Elefanten-Exuvie, in: Homann-Wedeking, E. and Segall, B. (eds.), Festschrift Eugen v. Mercklin. Waldsassen/Bayern, 152-162.

Scullard, H.H. 1974
The Elephant in the Greek and Roman World. London.

Slej, K. 1995
Kronprins Christian Frederik som Antiquar. Christian Frederiks vandringer i det antikke Rom

1819-1821 og mødet med to af Roms førende Antiquarer, in: Andersen, H.D., Cordsen, A., Horsnæs, H.W. and Slej, K. (eds.), Klassisk arkæologiske studier 2. København, 273-276.

Stribrny, K. 1991
Zur Entsethung der Elefanten-Exuvie als "Africa"-Attribut, in: Noeske, H.-C. and Schubert, H. (eds.), Die Münze. Bild – Botschaft – Bedeutung. Frankfurt am Main/Bern/New York/Paris, 378-385.

Svenson, D. 1995
Darstellungen hellenistischer Könige mit Götter attributen. Frankruft am Main 1995.

Topsøe-Jensen, T.A. and Marquard, E. 1935
Officerer i den Dansk-Norske Søetat 1660-1814 og den Danske Søetat 1814-1932 I. København.

Toynbee, J.M.C. 1973
Animals in Roman Life and Art. London/Southampton.

Zazoff, P. 1968
Etruskische Skarabäen. Mainz am Rhein.

Zazoff, P. 1983
Die antiken Gemmen, Handbuch der Archäologie. München.

Notes

1. I wish to thank Birthe and Steen Holck for their willingness to provide me with access to this most interesting documentary material, in the possession of the family. Helle Winge Horsnæs has been so kind as to verify that The Royal Collection of Coins and Medals does not include the coins received from Holck.

2. Jensen 1992, 20-27.

3. Jensen 1992, 25. For more information about Münter, cf. Breitenstein 1951, 59-60; Fischer-Hansen 1990, 170-175; Lund 1995, 200-202; Slej 1995, 277-278; Fischer-Hansen 1997 and 2009, and the literature cited in these sources. For more information about Georg Zoëga, cf. Andreasen and Ascani, 1967-2013, Krarup 1976 and Holm-Rasmussen 2001.

4. This letter is the oldest document in the archives of the National Museum's Collection of Classical and Near Eastern Antiquities; its receipt was acknowledged at the meeting of the Commission on the 10th of January 1811, cf. Jakobsen og Adamsen 2007, 221. I am grateful to Tove Jakobsen for referring me to Collegialtidende 1811, 27, and Indberetning I.254, Prot. no 1, 195, where mention is made of: "A female head, two feet and a hand of extraordinary size in marble. Found in the ruins of Utica … donated by Mr. captain Holck, knight of the Dannebrog". Anne Haslund Hansen 1999, 19-20, 48-50 notes that it

5. See Moltesen in the present publication.

6. Cf. Jensen 1992, 224-226.

7. Inv. no. ABb 102.

8. Inv. no. ABb 104.

9. Inv. no. ABb 107.

10. Inv. no. ABb 103. Length 17 cm.

11. Inv. no. ABb 105-106.

12. Inv. no. ABb 97. Breitenstein 1942; Rumpf 1963, 199; Sauer 1964, 158 note 29 pl. 55.1; Richter 1965, 255, no.5.a, fig.1724; Grimm 1978, 108 note 65.

13. Bosworth 1977; Grimm 1978, 108; Leclant and Clerc 1981; Kinast 1987.

14. Toynbee 1973, 50; Stribrny 1991, 379-380; Svenson 1995, 106-108.

15. SNG COP 40 pl. 1; Scullard 1974, 76 pl. 13.c; Mørkholm 1991, 63-65 no.90; Stribrny 1991; Stewart 1993, 434-435 and passim. In Late Hellenistic and Roman times, the elephant skin was regarded as an attribute of personifications of Africa, cf. Le Glay 1981.

16. Svenson 1995, 112-113. Cf. also Stewart 1993, 235-236.

17. Breitenstein 1941, 87-88.

18. According to Breitenstein 1981, 88 it is presumably "the ram's horns, which are apprehended as being wings, folded together, and to be sure, there are no traces of gilding now remaining, but the head seems to have been cleaned in the meantime, and it is quite possible that the preserved red

19. colour once served as an undercoating for the gilding".

20. This cupid's 'head of alabaster with gilded wings', brought back to Denmark by Falbe, inv. no. ABb 97, presumably vanished long before Breitenstein's day.

21. Feldbæk 1997.

22. Andersen 1996 and Andersen 2000.

23. Several of these people who made it home again published books about their days of hardship in the foreign lands, cf. Andersen 1995, 16-17; Rheinheimer 2001.

24. Wandel 1919, 1-4 and passim; Bjerg 1996; Andersen 2000, 245-249.

25. Wandel 1919.

26. Topsøe-Jensen and Marquard 1935, 590-592; Holck 1951; Marquard 1952, 456; Holck 1962; Andersen 1966 passim; Sørensen 1995, 63; Andersen 2000, 65. The miniature portrait is signed "Ioannes Patriarchi". In a letter from Copenhagen dated December 1, 1798, Henriette Holck writes, "I have come into possession of my dear Carl's portrait, and the resemblance is extraordinary – I am so very happy about it that I can hardly give words to it", cf. Holck 1951, 42-43. The colours on the forehead, the hair and the one eye were restored in the first half of the twentieth century.

27. Her given name at birth was Bolette Henriche Margrethe Lund (1776-1846). The miniature portrait is unsigned. It might

have been painted shortly after her wedding with Carl Christian in 1792, cf. Holck 1951, 3-4.

27. Andersen 1996, 13-15; Andersen 2000, 69-71.

28. Holck 1951, 20.

29. Holck 1951, 39.

30. Holck 1962.

31. Holck 1962, 74.

32. Holck 1962, 103-104.

33. Andersen 1966, 203 fig. 14.

34. Andersen 1962, 104.

35. Holck 1962, 113.

36. Holck 1962, 113.

37. Holck's diaries from Tunisia open up a window to this European microcosmos, which was not inert to intrigues, the formation of cliques and people talking behind each other's backs, cf. Holck 1962.

38. For the early archaeological exploration of Carthage, cf. Halbertsma 1991; Ciccotti 1999 and (published) 2000; Debergh 2000; Lund 1994; 2000 and 2005, with references to the older literary sources.

39. Cf. Hurst 1994, with additional references.

40. From Holck's hand-written "Mémoire sur Tunisie", in possession of the Royal Library.

41. As far as these quotations are concerned, cf. Holck 1996 passim.

42. Quoted from the journal of the National Museum's Collection of Classical and Near Eastern Antiquities.

43. Inv. no.110. Length 1.3 cm, width 1 cm.

44. The scarab was not included in Zazoff 1968. For more on Punic scarabs, cf. Zazoff 1983, 84-98; Redissi 1999, with additional references.

45. Inv. no.111, cornelian. Length 1.8 cm., width 1.5 cm.

46. Inv. no.113, magnetic ironstone. Length 1.6 cm., width 0.13 cm.

47. Inv. no.114, red jasper. Length: 2.7 cm., width 2.5 cm.

48. Inv. no.112, cornelian. Length 1.2 cm., width 1 cm.

49. In addition to the two "gems" in possession of the Collection of Classical and Near Eastern Antiquities, Carl Christian and Henriette Holck brought back with them two more pieces which have apparently disappeared, as well as three others which are still in the family's possession.

50. Cf. Halbertsma 1991 and Debergh 2005.

51. In the Collection of Manuscripts at the Royal Library.

52. Holck 1962, 102. Henriette Holck's illness is also a recurrent theme in the diaries covering the other years.

53. Marquard 1952, 457-458. Carl Christian's health was also so frail that in 1805 he was granted permission to travel to Italy, due to "total neurasthenia". In 1810, he was summoned home to Denmark, since "due to a lack of worldly knowledge" he did not always live in the desired accord with the other consuls.

54. Holck 1962, 101-102.

55. Holck 1962, 67-68; 115-116. At the beginning of 1806, inspiring a great deal of sorrow, they lost a daughter, only a few days after her birth.

56. In his "Memoire sur Tunis", Holck wrote that in much the manner of what one sees in Carthage, what you see "of the ruins of the famous Utica, which the Moors call Buschiator, are nothing else but ruins, a few cellars and a few cisterns".

57. Holck 1962, 122.

58. Gasparri 1986. According to Jakob Munk Højte, the wording of the inscription on the presumed pedestal is rather suggestive of an altar.

59. Niels Hannestad has drawn my attention to the fact that the fragments brought to Denmark by Holck conform to those parts, which he claims that the Muslims were in the habit of knocking off statues.

60. Holck 1962, 122.

61. Lund 2000b. In contrast to what Holck and Falbe did there, Gierlew collected almost no antique relics in Tunisia. Instead, he sent detailed descriptions about Carthage's topography to Frederik Münter in Copenhagen.

62. Lund 1986, 1992, 2000a, 2000c, 2008, 125-130 and 2014.

63. Peder Jonas Charisius might have been the first envoy to send antiques back to Denmark. See Anne Haslund Hansen's article in the present publication. Among the later exponents of this same tendency, there were Daniel Dumreicher, in Alexandria, cf. Buhl 1974, 20-25 and Julius Løytved, in Beirut, cf. Pentz in the present publication.

One God who vanquishes everything Evil
– a Syrian Amulet from the early Middle Ages

Peter Pentz

Many of the Syrian and West Asian articles that are part of the National Museum's Collection of Classical and Near Eastern Antiquities were donated by or purchased from Julius Løytved (1836 -1911). Julius Løytved, fig. 1 served as the Danish consul in Beirut from 1886 until 1897, but was already living in Syria and Lebanon from 1871.[1]

Løytved was not actually trained as an archaeologist or a historian, but he had an open and wide interest that cut across different times and different places. The character of Løytved's collections and acquisitions bears the imprint of this. A number of different departments in the National Museum have accordingly reaped the benefits of the consul's enterprise, these being the Ethnographic Collection, fig. 2, the Collection of Coins and Medals and, of course, the Collection of Classical and Near Eastern Antiquities. Outside the museum, there is also the Ny Carlsberg Glyptotek's Palmyra Collection, which is to a considerable extent another one of the fruits of Løytved's tireless efforts.

Fig. 1.
Julius Løytved (1836-1911), Danish consul in Beirut 1886-1897. Foto: The Royal Danish Library.

Fig. 2.
Turkish bath-sandals inlaid with mother-of-pearl, acquired by Julius Løytved. The Ethnographic Collection, the National Museum of Denmark, inv. Md. 97. Photo: The National Museum of Denmark.

A PRESUMABLY INCONSEQUENTIAL PIECE OF JEWELLERY

One of the less conspicuous articles for which the Collection of Classical and Near Eastern Antiquities can thank Julius Løytved is a rather small pendant made of bronze. In spite of its coarse and hardly refined manner of workmanship, this little piece of jewellery appears to be so well executed that it cannot be the work of an amateur.

The piece is oval, 4.5 centimetres high and decorated with a great many individual figures and inscriptions on both sides. The decorations are etched into the metal. The pendant has been supplied with an eye through which one could thread a chain or a leather strap in such a way that the article could be worn around the neck.

On the one side, we can see a rider with a halo, who is subjugating and penetrating a reclining creature with his lance, fig. 3. This creature looks something like a human being and the long hair could serve to indicate that what we have here before us is a woman. Beneath this rather anthropomorphic creature, there is an animal, with a mane that reveals that this must be a lion. An inscription with Greek letters at the top of the piece of jewellery appears to read: Εἷς Θεὸς Ὁ νικ'ν τὰ κακὰ, *One God who vanquishes everything evil.*

Fig. 3.
Pendant of bronze with incised horseman and inscription. A gift from Julius Løytved. The Collection of Classical and Near Eastern Antiquities, the National Museum of Denmark. Photo: The National Museum of Denmark.

Fig. 4.
Reverse of pendant, fig. 3, with an incised eye and inscription.

It is somewhat more difficult to identify the figures on the other side of the bronze plate, fig. 4. The central figure appears to be an almond-shaped human eye. On this side of the amulet, above the eye, there is also an inscription: ΙΑω ϹΑΒΑω ΜΙΧΑΗΛ ΒΟΗΘ(Ι), *Iaô, Sabaôth, Michaêl, help.* Above this inscription, a number of other figures can be seen: all the way to the left there is a lion – standing erect, then there is a bird which has to be deciphered as an ibis or a stork, with a serpent, a scorpion and all the way on the right and above the eye, a number of figures that cannot immediately be identified.

It is impossible to pinpoint precisely how old the amulet is. However, taking into account the rider with his halo and the invocation of a single God, the Greek letters situate the piece somewhere in the vicinity of the fifth, sixth, or seventh century AD.

THE EYE

The pendant in the Collection of Classical and Near Eastern Antiquities, however, is anything but unique. Generally speaking, it appears to be so that rider amulets were popular items in the Judeo-Christian tradition, fig. 5. What is even more surprising, however, is that the apparently casual accumulation of figures and sym-

Fig. 5.
Amulet of hematite with a depiction of Solomon and an inscription on the reverse: "The key of Solomon". Kelsey Museum of Archaeology, University of Michigan, inv. 26092. Acquired in Egypt. Photo: Kelsey Museum.

Fig. 6.
Bronze amulet, obverse and reverse, almost identical with fig. 3. Kelsey Museum of Archaeology, University of Michigan, inv. 26115. Syria. Photo: Kelsey Museum.

bols on the Løytved amulet appears on a number of similar amulets, all of which stem from Syria or elsewhere in the Middle East[2] and which can be found today in different collections and museums, fig. 6. The homogeneity among these accumulations is so striking that one could be led into believing either that they were copied, one after the other, or that they all fulfilled one and the same purpose.

With this piece of jewellery's almost *emblematic* content, it appears to be obvious that what we have before us is something other than pure ornamentation. It would rather have to be a matter of symbols; this is suggested especially by the magic eye.

The eye can be interpreted as either *the evil eye,* from which one ought to be protected, or the all-monitoring and protecting eye. It is being assaulted by different beings, each of which symbolises some kind of threat or other – certainly directed toward the person wearing the piece of jewellery, which must consequently be construed as an *amulet.* In other words, this is indeed an amulet. The word *amulet* stems from a Latin locution that signifies a *way of protecting oneself.*

The written sources frequently mention the eye and here it always seems to be evil or menacing to life and health.[3] The practice of symbolising the eye as evil or protective is considerably older than the amulet and harks back to the Egyptian tradition. Conversely, the symbol has persevered up to the present day. For these reasons, the eye must be regarded as a universal symbol. The amulet's other figures, which appear to be contesting the eye's power, are also familiar from older times. The bird is accordingly known from other amulets, interpreted here as an ibis. It is sometimes combined with a poisonous snake, supposedly referring to a tradition where the capability of neutralising the effect of poison – symbolised by the serpent[4] – was attributed to the ibis. One could also be tempted into believing that one of the maladies or dangers that the amulet was supposed to guard against was the effect of being poisoned.

Whatever threats or helping powers the other figures symbolise is unclear. The entirety in the presentation is known from a painted representation in Palmyra, where one of the decorations inside the so-called *Hypogea of the Three Brothers* shows the magic or evil eye, threatened by the same animals as we see on the amulet, fig. 7.[5] The Palmyrian grave has been dated to the second half of the

Fig. 7.
Painting in the "Hypogea of the Three Brothers" in Palmyra, after Colledge, M.A.R., The Art of Palmyra, London 1976, p. 85, fig. 48.

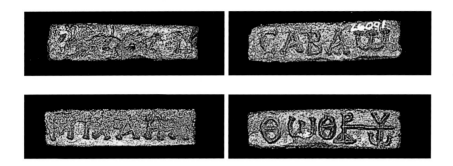

Second Century and is therefore considerably older than the diminutive piece of jewellery. From the painting, one can conclude, moreover, that the figures which cannot be deciphered on the amulet, must be pointed weapons – sword, daggers, a fork or spear – that point at the eye. This, of course, coincides neatly with the hypothesis that the eye is being threatened and these figures must accordingly be interpreted as the wearer of the ornament's protectors – against the evil eye. Moreover, the scenario is not totally unfamiliar in certain burial contexts we know about in two rock tombs in Al-Jish (in Palestine) from the Sixth Century, where the apotropaic (evil-averting) figures and texts, however, are not painted but are indeed found on amulets.[6]

The inscriptions have the character of an invocation: *Iaô, Sabaôth, Michaêl, help.* The combination of the two names for God, Iaô and Sabaôth, with the archangel Michael is known from another amulet, a small glass ingot or prism [7] with inscriptions on the ingot's four long sides, fig.8. The ingot's fourth side, however, is not inscribed with "help", but rather with the name *Tôth,* the Egyptian deity. This god is also found on amulets, fig. 9, where Toth is shown with the ibis head and the serpent's head and where the amulet is supposedly protecting the wearer against poisonings and stomach pains.[8] That the Egyptian god makes an appearance in the company of three Jewish names can perhaps be explained by the fact that Toth seems to have lived on further in the Greek mythology as Hermes, and Toth has also been construed as Moses.

SOLOMON THE MAGICIAN

On the other side of the piece of jewellery, as has been mentioned, we see a rider – with a halo – who impales a reclining and supposedly female figure. The rider appears on many amulets, fig. 5, both with and without halo. On a number of the amulets, it appears that the rider ought to be perceived as Solomon. In the Christian, the Jewish and the Islamic (as the Prophet Suleiman) traditions, Solomon is the sage and the magician.[9] In the apocryphal *Testament of Solomon,*

he actually appears as a *necromancer* in medieval fashion, replete with conjurations and invocations of demons like the female Lilith (Obizuth). The amulet's reclining female figure must accordingly be perceived as a demon.

In *The Testament of Solomon,* the sage calls upon the demons and compels them to reveal what their *counter-force* is.[10] In the instance of Lilith, it is the archangel Afarol (Rafael), and not Michael, who is the one being invoked on the amulet of the Collection of Classical and Near Eastern Antiquities'.[11] For every force or threat, then, there is an opposing counterpart. Solomon is the one who is capable of maintaining the balance between the two forces and of locking this in place with the aid of Solomon's seal or Solomon's key, fig. 5, notions that are known to us from the Medieval magic's world of ideas (one of the Middle Ages' magic books actually conveyed the name, *Solomon's Key*) and which lives on, all the way up to our time.

Representations of riders where the horseman gets the better of a dragon, a demon or some other foe must generally be apprehended as a kind of *psychomaki* and the rider's identity is not exclusively conjoined with that of Solomon. St. George is another well-known rider from the Christian iconography. What is interesting, however, is that it appears that the inscription *Solomon* on rider amulets can be seen on the relatively older examples and that the inscription comes eventually to be superseded by the rather bombastic declaration: One God who vanquishes everything evil.[12] The proposition has to be regarded as an expression of an intensely monotheistic attitude. Whether this consequently entails that the glorified rider on our amulet has to be apprehended as God himself is, however, uncertain.[13] An amulet of glass paste, found in Anemurium in Asia Minor, bears an inscription that reads: "Solomon's seal binds the evil eye".[14]

Parrying-off inscriptions like those seen on the amulet are familiar to us, moreover, in connection with the architecture of the period. Magical and protective inscriptions from the Fifth and Sixth centuries are not uncommon on residential dwellings from the so-called "dead cities" between Hama and Aleppo in Syria. These inscriptions, which are placed on the lintels over the main entrance doors, very often contain the wording "only one God"[15] and some of these inscriptions are directed, quite precisely, against the evil eye.[16]

A MAGICAL OBJECT

The piece of jewellery that Consul Løytved acquired in Syria is, then, not only a piece of jewellery – if it is a piece of jewellery at all. Rather than being beautiful and a delight to the eyes, it fulfilled the purpose of protecting its wearer against different kinds of threats.

An amulet of this kind is not merely an object with magic symbolic content; it is a magical object in itself.

The amulet is the physical manifestation of a black magician's rites and experiments. We can imagine that the magician has etched the figures into the amulet during certain rituals and while declaiming certain specific conjurations. This would explain the simple execution; it is also clear that the figures had to be etched successively, in concord with some kind of ritual or other.[17]

Such a practice is familiar to us from the late Middle Ages, where articles and inscriptions were *consecrated* during particular rituals and the declamation of different kinds of invocations, which typically were corrupted renditions of the established liturgical ones.

In this way, the amulet is presumably an example of how rituals that were considered the exclusive domain of the church, were put to use and thereby perverted and transgressed appointed moral boundaries – and consequently came into conflict with the church's wishes. However, to some extent, a continuity can be seen from the early *Christian* black magic to the practice of exorcism, which eventually came to be a well-established part of the accepted medieval liturgy.

The relatively young Christian Church, which preceded the date of the amulet's fabrication, of course, was on the lookout to suppress any kind of magic. *Necromancy* – black magic – was under an intense criticism put forward by prominent Christians. The Apostle Paul had already attempted to stamp out magic; in *The Acts of the Apostles,* it is told that he arrived in Ephesus and converted many of the city's inhabitants. "Many of them which also used curious arts" substantiated their devotion to the new faith through the means of a powerful demonstration. They "brought their books together and burned them before all men: and they counted the price of them, and found it fifty thousand pieces of silver",[18] a sum which also sets Judas's reward for the betrayal in striking relief.

Later on, other eminent ecclesiastic authorities such as Johannes Chrysostomos denounced the use of amulets and also, with more or less conviction, cast doubt on the belief that one person could harm another through the agency of the evil eye.[19]

On the one hand, Løytved's amulet points back in time and over to the appreciable legacy which the more populist faith had carried along from the pre-Christian era, as manifest with, for example, the ibis,[20] while simultaneously pointing forward in time, with its obvious similarity to the rituals that are known from the magicians' praxis of the late Medieval period.

Bibliography

Barb, A. A. 1972
Magica varia. Syria XLIX,
343-370.

Bonner, C. 1950
Studies in Magical Amulets, chiefly
Graeco-Egyptian. Ann Arbor:
University of Michigan Press,
1950. (University of Michigan
studies, Humanistic ser.; 49).

Bonner, C. 1951
Amulets chiefly in The British
Museum, Hesperia, 20, 301-345.

Bonner, C. 1954
A miscellany of engraved stones,
Hesperia, 23, 138-157.

Buhl, M.-L. 1977
Some Western-Asiatic bronze
figurines and a few remarks on
Julius Løytved as an antiquarian.
Acta Archaeologica, vol. 48,
139-154.

Colledge, M.A.R. 1976
The Art of Palmyra. London.

Dickie, M. W. 1995
The Fathers of the Church and the
Evil Eye, 9-34 in Henry Maguire
ed, Byzantine Magic. Dumbarton
Oaks.

Duffy, J. 1995
Reactions of Two Byzantine
Intellectuals to the Theory and
Practice of Magic: Michael Psellos
and Michael Italikos, 83-95 in
Henry Maguire ed, Byzantine
Magic. Dumbarton Oaks.

Flint, V. I. J. 1991
The Rise of Magic in Early
Medieval Europe, Princeton:
Princeton University Press.

Gager, J. G. 1992
Curse Tablets and Binding Spells
from the Ancient World, Oxford:
Oxford University Press.

Maguire, H. 1995
Byzantine Magic, edited by
Henry Maguire, Papers from
a 1993 Colloquium. Harvard
University Press/Dumbarton Oaks
Research Library and Collection,
Washington, D.C.

Michel, S. 1995
Medizinisch-magische
Amulettgemmen der Antike.
Schutz und Heilung durch Zauber
und edle Steine,
Antike Welt 26, Heft 5, 379-387.

Michel, S. 2002
Simone Michel: Seele,
Finsternis, Schutzgottheit und
Schicksalsmacht: der Pantheos auf
magischen Gemmen, Vorträge aus
dem Warburg-Haus, Band 6, 1-40.

Michel, S. 2004
Die Magischen Gemmen. Zu
Bildern und Zauberformeln
auf geschnittenen Steinen der
Antike und Neuzeit.
Studien aus dem Warburg-Haus,
Band 7.

Michel von Dungern, S. 2012
Abracadabra Abraxas. Magie und
Zauberei in der Heilkunde der
römischen Zeit. Broschüre zur
gleichnamigen Sonderausstellung.
Museum Malerwinkelhaus, 29.
März – 04. November.

Naveh, J. & Shaul Shaked 1985
Amulets and Magic Bowls:
Aramaic Incantations of Late
Antiquity, Jerusalem: Magnes Press.

Naveh, J. & Shaul Shaked, 1993
Magic Spells and Formulae:
Aramaic Incantations of Late
Antiquity, Jerusalem: Magnes Press.

Prentice, W.K. 1906
Magical Formulae of Lintels of
the Christian Period in Syria.
American Journal of Archaeology,
vol. 10, 137-150.

Russell, J. 1982
The Evil Eye in Early
Byzantine Society, Jahrbuch der
Österreichischen Byzantinischen
Gesellschaft, Wien, 32.3.
(Akten XVI Internationaler
Byzantinistenkongress, II,3).

Russell, J. 1995
The Archeological Context of
Magic in the Early Byzantine
Period, 35-50 in: Henry Magiure
ed, Byzantine Magic. Dumbarton
Oaks.

Seyrig, H. 1934
Invidiae medici. Berytus I, 1-11.

Notes

1   Buhl 1977, 154.

2   A rapid survey of the publications brings the number up to around twenty-five examples (see Bonner 1950, 50ff, plate IV, D 77-82 and Barb 1972, 358 note 1). The real quantity of extant examples would have to be significantly greater. For examples that came to light subsequent to Bonner's and Barb's publications, see Russell, 1995, 40, n. 17. The amulet that is depicted as fig. 6, (Kelsey 26115)(Bonner 1950, no. 299) is one of the examples that most resembles the one in possession of the Collection of Classical and Near Eastern Antiquities.

3   See, for example, Duffy, 1995 and Dickie, 1995. – On "the evil eye" in the early Medieval Byzantine world, see Russell, 1982 and Russell, 1995, 37ff, n. 5 37.

4   Barb 1972, 361. The serpent as a symbol of poison lives on further through the developing iconography of the Middle Ages, for example, when one sees a serpent in the cup of John.

5   I owe a debt of gratitude to Professor P. J. Riis for this cross-reference.

6   For references to examples found at graves from Jordan and Palestine, with evil-averting depictions and texts, see Russell, 1995, 44-45.

7   Bonner 1950, no. 361.

8   Bonner 1950, no. 264.

9   For Solomon's role in magic in the early Christian period, in general, see Russell, 1995, 39, n. 15.

10 According to descriptions in Medieval books of magic, this was an entirely ordinary practice.

11 On the archangels' role in early Christian magic, see Russell, 1995, 41 and note 22 on the same page. Similarly, the eye and the monotheist "One God" appear on lintels over the doors of Syrian houses from the Fifth and Sixth centuries. Moreover, the archangels are named, every now and then, in the protective inscriptions (see, for example, Prentice, 1906, 143).

12 Barb 1972, 350 note 5.

13 Bonner (1950, 210f) holds the opinion that the rider is Christ. A Syrian amulet or medallion in the Kelsey Museum (Kelsey Museum 26115) shows a glorified rider, who subdues a recumbent demon or person, with a quotation from *The Book of Psalms* (*The Book of Psalms,* 91) inscribed: "He that dwelleth in the secret place of the most High shall abide under the shadow of the Almighty. I will say of the Lord…"; this quotation can be found on many early Christian and Jewish amulets and the reeling off of the threats in *The Book of Psalms,* 91, with the explicit enumeration of the lion, the adder and the dragon, corresponds to the picture rendered on the Collection of Classical and Near Eastern Antiquities' amulet. On the verso side of Kelsey 26115, we can read: "Holy, holy, holy Sabaoth. The living God's Seal, protect from everything evil the wearer of this amulet!" (Bonner 1950, no. 324). Here, it appears that God himself has taken the place of Solomon and that Solomon's seal has come to be God's seal. On another amulet (Royal Ontario Museum 986.181.123), which also bears the inscription from *The Book of Psalms,* the verso, however, features an image of an archangel holding a Crucifix-staff and the orb of the world, presumably Michael (see http://www.rom.on.ca/galleries/byzantine/byzammichael.html). The amulets, then, appear to be moving around in a truly homogenous universe of quotations, gods, saints, angels and *characteres*.

14 Russell, 1995, 39.

15 Prentice, 1906, 139; Russell, 1995, 38.

16 Saqqa, dated 546 (Prentice, 1906, 141).

17 A physician of the Sixth Century, Alexander of Tralles, offers a detailed account of an amulet ring and the conjurations, prayers and magic symbols which have to be included herein (Duffy, 1995, 95). Moreover, what comes to light in this text is that the knowledge that was required for preparing the ring was not intended for everyone.

18 *The Acts of the Apostles,* 18:19-19:20.

19 On the Fathers of the Church, see Dickie, 1995, especially 9-11. On Johannes Chrysostomos and "the evil eye" see: Dickie, 1995, especially 21-24; Russell, 1995, 38, n. 10.

20 Cf. Seyrig 1934.

A Valley in the Zagros Mountains
– the Danish Expedition to Luristan

Henrik Thrane

On a beautiful April day in 1963, five Danes sat in a chaikhané and let themselves glide forth into the spirit of the Persian lifestyle by listening to the cool running water coming down from the mountains and flowing through the canal that ran right through the middle of the teahouse courtyard, fig. 1. In a country that is virtually scorched by the sun on most days of the year, the garden, the water and the shadow are natural elements in representations of Paradise.

The teahouse was situated on the road dating from time immemorial – the Silk Road – which has connected East and West since the dawn of culture. The very sound of the words, Silk Road, still gets many of us to prick up our ears and

Fig. 1.
A moment of rest in the teahouse at the foot of Bisutun, with the members of the expedition seated in the shadow, in the background. Photographed by Jørgen Meldgaard on April 10, 1963.

dream about caravans with silk and other precious wares, about deserts and adventures. Here, at the 400-metre high Bisutun (or Behistun) rock, with its view over the expansive fertile plain between Hamadan and Kermanshah to the north of the Zagros Mountains' solid mass, the Persian king Dareios ordered the cutting of the renowned relief representing himself as the triumphator receiving vanquished and pinioned prisoners, and with the rather conceited accompanying inscription in three languages, which came to establish the point of origin of Assyriology.

So here we sat and charged our energies for the expedition into the unknown territory – Luristan. Once again, a name with an almost magical ring to it.

We were young. Only two of us had breathed Persian air before. The task before us was ambitious. As the newspapers had written, we were supposed to solve the enigma of a unique culture, which had created, in this harsh and rugged mountainous region, an imaginative and fantastic form of bronze art. Over the course of thirty years, these bronzes had come to be one of the favourite topics of conversation in the international art market. The problem was that nobody had *seen* Luristan bronzes in their own milieu – they had only been spotted in the dealers' rags and display cases. Where did they come from? How old were they? Who had made them and who had used them? No scholar had managed to penetrate into the place where the Lurs shovelled them up presumably from ancient graves. All the information came from third-hand sources – or more remotely. Through one entire generation, Frenchmen and Englishmen had attempted to procure proper information – without any luck. Now it was our turn! But why Danes? Not since Carsten Niebuhr's journey had any Dane carried out research into ancient Persian archaeology.

The reason was simple: Coincidence – or fortunate circumstances. As part of the Shah of Iran's modernisation of the enormous and often impassable country, a strategic main road was planned along the border with Iraq, running the length of the Zagros Mountains, which extend all the way from Turkey (Kurdistan) to the Persian Gulf like a formidable barrier between the two vast plains, Mesopotamia and the Iranian flatlands. The Silk Road's route past Qasr-i Shirin was, by and large, the only proper link between the two areas north of the Saimarreh River's breach south of Susa. Smugglers were the only ones who dared to roam across the hidden passes connecting these two routes.

Danish construction engineers based in Iran working for the firm Kampsax, with long experience in Iran, were entrusted with the task of building the new road and it was Kampsax that volunteered to underwrite the expenses of an archaeological effort. The engineers could see how the road was moving past – or right through – one burial ground after another and they observed how ancient pottery and bronzes were being peddled in enormous quantities. Both for the enterprise and as far as our presence in the region was concerned, the fact that no strategic interest in this part of the eternally keyed-up Middle East could be imputed to Denmark as a small nation, was not inconsequential.

The Carlsberg Foundation paid the costs of our travel (and subsequently carried the load further, paying for the processing of the finds and the publication thereof). Kampsax covered all the expenses in Iran and placed at our disposal two factory-fresh Land Rovers, with Iranian chauffeurs. In the shadow of the Saimarreh Bridge, the little house that we dubbed Fort Saimarreh was newly furnished as the headquarters of the National Museum's Luristan expedition, fig. 2.

The team consisted of curator Mr. Imani from the Iranian Department of Antiquities; architect Erik Ejrnæs; assistant keeper Peder Mortensen from the Collection of Classical and Near Eastern Antiquities; archaeology student Erik Brinch Petersen; the author of the present article, a research fellow at the time; and the leader of the group, assistant curator Jørgen Meldgaard from the Ethnographic Collection. In 1962, Meldgaard had been sent to the region by the state antiquary, P.V. Glob, and as a result of his scouting along the lapse of the "Road", he had chosen, among several other suitable spots, a small mound called Tepe Guran. Here,

Fig. 2.
The bridge over the Saimarreh River, seen here from the southwest, is the largest of the engineering projects on the road through Luristan. On the left, on the river's left bank, there is a small house near the waterside that was re-furbished to accommodate the members of the expedition. Notwithstanding snakes on the roof and scorpions we might encounter on the way to the loo, this house served as a cosy frame around our evenings and our leisure time. Looking to the north, on the left, there is the so-called 'service road', which was the one we had to drive on; the asphalt for the proper road had not yet been poured. The road crosses over an ancient cemetery – Shir-i Chigha. Photographed by the author on April 12, 1963.

Fig. 3.
The view from Bisutun's tri-lingual inscription, looking south down toward Harsin, where the Saimarreh River winds its way through narrow ravines down towards the Hulailan Plain and where the Luristan bronzes first appeared on the market in the 1920s. Tepe Sarab is not far from Bisutun. Photographed by the author on April 10, 1963.

it appeared there might be a chance to find graves from the conjectured Luristan Bronze Age culture. Moreover, there were traces from the early Neolithic period.

From Bisutun, we had been looking down at Tepe Sarab, a recently excavated, small tepe with traces of a very early agriculture – which topic was also scheduled to be an object of our investigation, fig. 3. In the 1950s and 1960s, there was a boom of interest in this archaeological period; the hunt for the earliest agricultural settlement was quite intense at the time. With focused determination, American archaeologists had been working along the southern face of the Zagros Mountains – and they were obtaining good results. There was a kind of race going on. And on every lap, the early farmers moved a few centuries further back in time. Now Peder Mortensen was going to try his luck, while I was assigned to dig in search of the "Bronze" graves.

Tepe Guran was not a particularly large tepe, fig. 4, measuring only 60 × 120 metres. However, its dolichocephalic dome prominently asserted itself across the expanse of the surrounding plain. The Tepe was situated at the edge of a small river, Yazman Rud, which flowed into Luristan's principal artery, the Saimarreh River. Tepe Guran was located at the northwest edge of the Hulailan Plain, which the waters of the Saimarreh make into one of Luristan's most productive plains, fig. 5.

Surveys in 1962, 1964 and 1974-75 and again in 1977 have together created a picture of the settled areas existing in ancient times on the plain which now stands as one of the most detailed in the entire Middle East. Peder Mortensen was able to trace cultural fluctuations all the way back to the Early Stone Age –

Fig. 4.
Tepe Guran, as seen from
the east, with the expedi-
tion's tent at the top and
the Neolithic excavation
on the slope. Bronze Age
and Iron Age layers are
found on the flattened end,
at the left. The people from
the village of Guran are
about to pitch the year's
first camp at the annual
circuit-tour in the terrain,
in order to procure feed for
the livestock. In the course
of the year, the residents
of the village of Guran
moved out into the black
tents on their annual cir-
cuit-tour up around in the
mountains. The old noma-
dic life was documented in
1964 by Lennart Edel-
berg, who was able to plot
out the old Lur calendar's
yearly cycle with four pha-
ses. Photographed by the
author on May 25, 1963.

Fig. 5.
The Hulailan Plain, as
seen from the southwest.
Photographed by the au-
thor on May 17, 1963.

Fig. 8.
The flagstones covering T 11 had cracked and fallen down into the tomb's cavity. As part of this process, the intact and the shattered pots also fell down and were discovered lying with their mouths facing down. Seen from the north. Photographed by the author on June 11, 1963.

identified). The garments were not of the coarse woollen kind that we know about from Bronze Age oak coffins here in Denmark, but rather of linen.

Tripod-based vessels, cooking utensils and storage vessels, along with a great many goblets, were part of every grave, partly as accessories accompanying the corpse, partly deposited or thrown onto the covering flagstones (figs. 7-8).

There was an analogous situation at the oldest of the graves found in the southern excavation, fig. 9. Here lay a woman with a bronze cup, clay vessels, two clothing pins and a toe-ring! Her drinking vessels were of a different type than what we found in burials T 9, 11 & 15, fig. 10. These vessels belong to a group that is known from both Mesopotamia and the Zagros Mountains, which is denoted "Khabur cups". We encounter these items in scattered tombs of the same type as T 19. Nobody knows how to explain this phenomenon. The datings are very broad in scope and since we cannot connect T 19 directly with the graves on the top of Tepe Guran, a dating to around 1400 BC is, for all intents and purposes, a guess. The cups in T 19 display elegant forms, which in all likelihood are foreign originals as well as local imitations. Whether or not the deceased person's family lived in Tepe Guran is not known. The cups are rare, also here in Luristan, and actual settlements with them are unknown.

After some time without any trace of human activity, it appears that a house was built on top of T 19, *not* containing Khabur ceramics but nonetheless replete with painted clay vessels. The small segment excavated is just a fragment of a house with mudbrick walls and wall- and floor-plastering. It is the tradition from the Stone Age that we observe here.

Fig. 9.
T 19 was unearthed on the last two days that Peder Mortensen and I were on Tepe Guran. The other members of the expedition had already driven on to Teheran, but we still had some things to finish up. The grave was excavated from the end that extended right into the small excavation area, seen here from the east. Photographed by the author on June 20, 1963.

Fig. 10.
Cups of the "Khabur type" from T 19, with the characteristically simple painting of narrow bands. The largest of the cups is 9.4 cm. high. Photo by Lennart Larsen.

The following settlement brought forth an entirely new kind of pottery and a new kind of architecture. Now, the houses were built with walls (or in any event, with foundations) of boulders, and this is a tradition that continues for as long as anyone resides at this spot. The pottery is characterised by a new kind of drinking vessel, tall goblet-like cups, which seem to be as rare in Luristan as the "Khabur cups", fig. 11. And like the latter, the goblets offer testimony about far-reaching connections extending *beyond* the mountains – with the trend-setting cultures. Whether the goblets should be set into connection with the Elamite culture, with its centre in Susa – south of Luristan, or with the Kassite dynasty in Mesopotamia poses a tickling problem. Both of these cultures made use of almost the same kinds of clay-vessel forms – a manifestation of the close, if not always exactly peaceful, relations between these two cultural centres. We know the Kassites more from their written sources and less from the archaeological items they left behind. It is presumed that these people came from the Zagros Mountains, so a connection pointing back to them seems reasonable. Although I am of the opinion that the Kassite connection is the most probable, conclusive evidence is missing. Maybe it will turn up with further analyses of the clay in the goblets and in cross-comparisons with Susa and Kassite goblets and also with local deposits of clay in the two regions. One attempt has been initiated, but this kind of investigation requires a larger international effort than is possible at the present time. What the appearance of the *foreign* pottery in this corner of the Hulailan Plain signifies is debatable.

The distinctive potshapes may have been brought by a group of people who built an outpost for themselves here and who had a need to maintain their civilised status. One need only think about how Chinese people and Englishmen brought along the indispensable tea set or how difficult it was for the Romans to make do without their wine serving accessories.

After a few rather uninteresting habitation layers, there was a layer from a burned-down complex of buildings. This layer was badly marred by "robbers' nests" and tomb T 4, fig. 12. We assume that the two partially excavated smaller rooms were independent entities, since we found almost the same repertoire of pots in both of them. The bad luck of the past comes to be the good fortune of the archaeologist; here, there lay an entire set of clay vessels, storage vessels, cooking pots and an elegant little teapot-like pitcher with a long spout. We are able to date this piece, employing a comparison with other well-dated, equally characteristic pitchers. This brings us near the end of the second millennium, supposedly around 1000 BC.

The dating is important, because it fixes a date before the construction of a small cemetery, which was dug right down into this habitation layer. Where exactly the people were living, whether it was right on Tepe Guran or at some other settlement in the near vicinity, cannot be determined as yet. The situation

Fig. 11.
Goblet from the "Kassite"
layer. Height: 19.2 cm.
Photo by Lennart Larsen.

Fig. 12.

Fig. 12.
'T' 4 during the excavation
process, while the flagstones
were still in place, but
with the "dromos" cleared
of earth, as seen from the
south. On the right, and
in the foreground, the
burned house can be seen.
Photographed by Jørgen
Meldgaard on April 27,
1963.

is the same as it was with the earliest burials on Guran's top and T 19. Since we have only unearthed 1.3% of Tepe Guran, there is room enough for houses and graves from the missing periods to turn up, even houses that were contemporary with the discovered graves. That is the drawback with soundings: they cannot provide this kind of information.

The most beautiful and most interesting of all the four stone cists was T 4, fig. 12. Inside this tomb lay an adult male, on his left side, with bent legs and arms on a kind of bed formed by four square sun-baked mudbricks. At his feet, there was a bronze cup of the same form as the ceramic cups found in the graves at the barrow's top, as well as a small bronze pitcher with an extremely long spout and a remnant of roasted mutton – another remnant of roasted mutton lay at the knees. At the spot where the belt would be worn, there was a bronze dagger. Around the wrists, there were iron bracelets and on many of the fingers were rings, all

made of iron. There are plain finger rings as well as some wider ones, which in other finds have incised images and, in all likelihood, functioned as signets. Rust prevents us from seeing whether the rings in T 4 had this function. Presumably worn around the neck, there were a total of sixteen beads of cornelian.

This combination of bronzes and iron ornaments is typical of an early Iron Age culture. The other three stone cists display the same combination and are supplied with pins and knives of iron as well as an abundant set of beads in one of the women's graves.

Curiously enough, we are not far away, in time, from the final phase of our own Nordic Bronze Age, which evinces the very same mixture of these two metals – bronze and iron.

The cemetery was covered over by a new layer of houses with a kind of ceramics that is difficult to situate. Quite simply, any standard of comparison is missing. The houses had been constructed in what had by now come to be an age-old tradition, with stone walls, as we still see in the modern Luri traditional winter house – the "zemga".

Fig. 14.
Luristan and the Lurs
came to take on the cha-
racter of a "life event" for
those of us who had the
good fortune to experience
their company before re-
volution and war turned
everything upside down.
A social revolution was in
the making at the time we
arrived. But we saw the final days of the patriarchal
lifestyle and we experien-
ced a group of people who
had not been cowed by
their conditions. Regardless
of how romantic they ap-
peared to us, who were
coming from the social
welfare state so far away,
they were living under
tough circumstances. Not-
withstanding the hardships
they faced, they did their
utmost to accommodate us
with kindness and lived
up to the high standards of
Eastern hospitality. Photographed by the author on
May 23, 1963.

Fig. 15.
Among the upper class, the earthly rendition of paradise was unfolded, according to one's means. Shady divans and rose-fragrant gardens with running water in the canals, where you could read the Persian classics and smoke your pipe in the shade of the sun, represent an exquisite ideal. These garden layouts are already known from the first Persian kings' grandiose garden layout in Pasargadae; they have placed their mark on Persian architecture ever since. This rendition was the frame for the last descendant of Pish-i Kuh's wali (absolute ruler), Khan Hussein Pur Abu Qaddareh, seen here on the left in his long black abba next to Jørgen Meldgaard. Photographed by Peder Mortensen on June 13, 1963.

The latest of the graves was dug down through the last layer of settlement and was nothing more than a pit, where a mature man, whose teeth and gums were in a very poor condition, was stretched out on his back with his short sword and a spearhead, both made of iron, as well as the last rendition of the same kind of drinking cup that has already been mentioned a number of times – a tenacious tradition, inasmuch as we can presume that this warrior was buried around 700 BC. There was no visible sign of violence. But death need not be violent, even for warriors. What I imagine is that he came to Hulailan with a detachment of troops, which marched through the mountains in one of the great many conflicts which are known to us from the Assyrians' concise reports about campaigns into the Zagros Mountains. There appear to be no finds on Tepe Guran from the time of the Assyrians, although there are a good many imported objects and other testimonies to Assyrian influence elsewhere in Luristan.

Some of the potsherds belong to the time of the Persian Wars, but cannot be set into connection with any proper buildings. The most recent trace of life on Tepe Guran is a small and presumably late, almost contemporary, Islamic burial place, which we successfully managed to dig our way around.

The presumed 700-800 years of building settlements we were able to document on the Bronze and Iron Ages' Tepe Guran were not exactly characterised by stability. Burials alternated with houses and it does not appear that any continuity for more than a few generations at a time was the norm. Nonetheless, despite the time differences and the interruptions in the occupation periods here, there are many features evincing a surprising constancy through the centuries: stone cists, cooking pots, the large storage vessels with ribbon-like mouldings, the small drinking cups, mutton meat in the graves are all found from the Bronze Age and onward, through the entire course of the temporal space where we can follow the usage of Tepe Guran.

If one has seen the nomads in the simple and nonetheless quite refined black tents, it may be difficult to extricate himself from a sense that it must have *always* been this way for these people. Nature calls for a shifting exploitation, conditioned by the seasons' marked differences in temperature and plant growth. However, nomadism is hardly a phenomenon going back to time immemorial, and it is very difficult to substantiate in a purely archaeological way: a tent leaves behind almost no traces in the terrain. It is quite conceivable that nomadism appeared at a number of *different* periods in prehistoric times. But on the basis of what we found at Tepe Guran, we are not able to substantiate its existence.

The fluctuations in the use of the tepe, of course, have to be considered in the light of the development, specifically, in the Hulailan Valley and, more generally, in this part of Luristan. The meticulous reconnaissance that Peder Mortensen carried out in 1974-77 provides a framework for a more comprehensive settlement history than our limited diggings permitted.

Our expedition's very restricted effort failed to solve the enigma of the Luristan bronzes, but it succeeded in bringing forth the first basic knowledge about the development in ceramics and building customs of a period which, prior to 1963, was absolutely undocumented in Luristan – and still is not very well known at all in the rest of Iran. One attempt to continue in 1964 wound up in disappointment. And the Islamic revolution in 1979 closed Luristan off once again to any foreign investigations and research.

The Danish stakes were minimal and the yield was optimal. I regard it as an object lesson of how a small country can make an important contribution for a relatively small amount of money, under the right conditions. However, as always in archaelogy a little bit of luck is indispensable.

a terracotta mould, one in the National Museum in Copenhagen, fig. 1, the other in the British Museum in London, actually join.[6]

In 1888 Wolfgang Helbig wrote to the National Museum enquiring if they had any of the terracottas from Taranto, as he said he was about to receive a shipment from Taranto.[7] The museum's reply is unknown, but Helbig, who paid his first visit to Copenhagen in that year to meet Brewer Carl Jacobsen, did sell a group of some 18 pieces to the National Museum.[8] The British Museum also acquired a series of pieces from Helbig in the same year.[9] The British Museum pieces were described as a "collection", while Breitenstein used the phrase a "collective find".[10] We may presume that all were in fact found together, but the precise location is unrecorded. One might perhaps suspect that the whole group was associated in some way with either the Giovinazzi or Pizzone finds, which were clearly still supplying terracottas to the market in the mid 1880s, if not also later. Nevertheless, Helbig's suggestion that he is about to receive a new consignment in early 1888 seems to suggest rather that the material was connected with the find in a well on private property in the area of the Borgo and briefly reported in that year.[11] Lippolis has plausibly associated this find with the discoveries in 1890, 1891 and 1898 on the via Anfiteatro. The 1888 find, as recorded by Luigi Viola, included fragments of skyphoi with painted inscriptions recording their association with a sanctuary of Dionysos (ιαρα Διονυσω): he mentions "molti frammenti di vasi rustici ed a vernice nera" and "con lettere dipinte in rosso ed in nero". The excavations of 1891 revealed black-glaze skyphoi with similar dipinto inscriptions in red slip, while work in 1898 uncovered traces of a monumental temple, dated by Lippolis to 450-350 BC.

The reunited mould, which is made from pale Apulian clay and measures 16.7 cms wide and more than 17.0 cms high, would have produced a very fine high relief head of a woman, set very nearly fully frontal, but with a very slight turn to her right, fig. 2.[12] She is full featured with loosely modelled wavy hair that is parted in the middle. She wears a chiton, which was pinned or buttoned at the shoulder and has a V-shaped neck line, a pair of earrings in the form of a rosette with an inverted pyramid pendant below, and a necklace that seems to have a central member that could have been intended to be a Herakles knot (a white grit has damaged the surface nearby). Her neck has two "Venus rings". On her head she also has an ivy wreath seemingly surmounted by a five-lobed fruit, rather than a rosette.[13] In the rectangular surround appear more fruit – two pomegranates at the top, and probably two quinces at the bottom. At the bottom of the mould is a horizontal groove with an angled one below, neither of which is easily explained. Nevertheless, in the light of such pieces as the fine mould from a cistern on the via Principe Amedeo in Taranto[14] and the votive plaque from Herakleia,[15] Taranto's daughter colony, we might imagine that the angled

Fig. 2.
The mould reunited. The
fragment in the British
Museum to the right.
Photo National Museum
of Denmark.

groove is actually one of her fingers and that the woman was shown holding some sort of tray or table, although no traces of offerings are preserved on the top. The date seems to be the third quarter of the fourth century.

The rectangular border and the fruit placed in the field indicate that the mould was not for an antefix.[16] It could, however, have been for a votive plaque, similar to the one from Herakleia, but its scale perhaps suggests that it was rather for one face of a small rectangular altar or incense burner of a type known from Taranto.[17] Indeed, Wuilleumier, who made the first listing of such objects, illustrated an example of similar size and with a similar frontal head, between pillars, which would seem to represent Aphrodite as there is an Eros on either side, fig. 3.[18] Many more examples are now known, including a type that is preserved in several versions, for which is also known a fragment of a mould, and seems to show a bride on a *kline*.[19] The most remarkable, however, is the pair of large altars in the J. Paul Getty Museum with connected scenes in relief showing Adonis and Aphrodite.[20]

The identity of the woman represented in our reunited mould is not easily determined. Firstly, if it is correct to interpret the lower edge as a hand holding a vessel or tray, we are presumably not dealing with a divine image but rather with a representation of an offerand, although the distinction is probably not always intended to be clear or real (either by the maker or to the consumer). The pomegranates and quinces suggest a connection with Persephone or Demeter, perhaps recalling the Hellenistic inscription naming a Karpophoros in Castella-neta not far to the northwest of Taranto, which itself suggests Demeter's cult title Malophoros at Selinus on Sicily.[21] There remains, however, the ivy wreath. This suggests a connection with Dionysos and so one might presume that it alludes here to some sort of a particular connection with the cult of Dionysos whose sanctuary seems to have been nearby.[22] Indeed, the other terracotta moulds in the Copenhagen group have several connections with Dionysos, especially those for a satyr and for a phallus.[23] The moulds in the British Museum have much in common with the Danish series, but also include examples of comic and tragic masks.[24]

Fig. 3.
Altar for burning incense.
Terracotta. From Taranto.
After P. Wuilleumier,
Tarente. 1939, Pl. XLII, 2.

Terracotta moulds found in a well with cult objects from a sanctuary of Dionysos suggest the presence of a workshop or workshops close by. Such a practical arrangement for the visitor to this and the other sanctuaries in the city and outside the walls, as well to the necropolises, no doubt accounts in part for the sheer quantity of votive terracottas preserved in Taranto. The little portable altar, or altars, that bore such a frontal female head as the reunited London and Copenhagen mould may well have had fruit placed on them as an offering to the goddess, but they could also have been used for burning incense.[25]

Bibliography

Bencze, A. 2013
Physionomies d'une cite grecque:
développpments stylistiques de la
coroplathie votive archaïque de
Tarente, Naples.

Bennett, M. J. et al. 2002
Magna Graecia: Greek Art
from Southern Italy and Sicily,
Cleveland.

Breitenstein, N. 1941
Catalogue of Terracottas, Cypriote,
Greek, Etrusco-Italian and Roman,
Copenhagen.

Burkert, W. 1985
Greek Religion, Cambridge, Mass.

Burkert, W. 1987
Ancient Mystery Cults,
Cambridge, Mass.

Carducci, C. A. A. 1771
Tommaso Nicolò d'Aquino. Delle
delizie tarentine libri IV con
versione e comment, Napoli.

Evans, A. J. 1886
Recent discoveries of Tarentine
terra-cottas, Journal of Hellenic
Studies 7, 8-23.

Herdejürgen, H. 1971
Die tarentinischen Terrakotten des
6. bis 4. Jahrhunderts v. Chr. im
Antikenmuseum Basel, Basel.

Herdejürgen, H. 1978
Götter, Menschen und Dämonen:
Terrakotten aus Unteritalien, Basel.

Higgins, R. A. 1954
Catalogue of Terracottas in the
British Museum, London.

Hinz, V. 1998
Der Kult von Demeter und Kore
auf Sizilien und in der Magna
Graecia, Wiesbaden.

Kingsley, B. M. 1976
The Terracottas of the Tarentine
Greeks: An Introduction to the
collection of the J. Paul Getty
Museum, Malibu.

Kingsley, B.M. 1979
The Reclining Heroes of Taras and
Their Cult, California Studies in
Classical Antiquity 12, 201-220.

Kingsley, B. M. 1981
Coroplastic Workshops at Taras:
Marked Moulds of the Late
Classical Period, J. Paul Getty
Museum Journal 9, 41-58.

Lenormant, F. 1881-1882
Notes archéologiques sur Tarente,
Gazette Archéologique 7, 148-190.

Lenormant, F. 1882
Les terre cuites de Tarente, Gazette
des Beaux-Arts 25, 201-224.

Lentini, C. (ed.) 1993
Un'arula tra Heidelberg e Naxos:
Atti del Seminario di studi
Giardini Naxos 18-19 ottobre
1990, Messina.

Lippolis, E. et al. 1995
Culti Greci in Occidente I:
Taranto, Taranto.

Lippolis, E. et al. 1996
Arte e artigianato in Magna
Grecia, Napoli.

Lippolis, E. 2001
Culto e iconografie della
coroplastica votive. Problemi
interpretative a Taranto e nel
mondo Greco, Mélanges de l'École
francaise de Rome, Antiquitè, 113,
225-255.

Lippolis, E. 2005
Practica rituale e coroplastica
votive a Taranto, in M.L. Nava
and M. Osanna (eds.), Lo Spazio
del Rito: Santuari e culti in Italia
Meridionale tra Indigeni e Greci,
Bari, 91-102.

Moltesen, M. 1987
Wolfgang Helbig: Brygger
Jacobsens Agent i Rom 1887-1914.
Copenhagen.

Moltesen, M. 2012
Perfect Partners: The Collaboration
between Carl Jacobsen and his
Agent in Rome Wolfgang Helbig

in the Formation of the Ny Carlsberg Glyptotek 1887-1914, Copenhagen.

Massar, N. 2008
Les thymiatèria dans le monde grec: état des lieux, in A. Verbanck-Piérard, N. Massar and D. Frère, Parfums de l'antiquité: la rose et l'encens en Mediterranée, Mariemont, 191-205.

Neutsch, B. 1967
Archäologische Studien und Bodensondierungen bei Policoro in den Jahren 1959-1964, in B. Neutsch et al., Archäologische Forschungen in Lukanien II: Herakleiastudien, Heidelberg.

Poli, N. 2010
Collezione Tarentino del Civico Museo di Storie e Arte di Trieste: Corpolastica Arcaica e Plastica, Trieste.

Salapata G. 2001
Τριφίλητος Ἄδωνις: An Exceptional Pair of Terracotta Arulae from South Italy, in M. True and M.L. Hart (eds.), Studia Varia from the J. Paul Getty Museum, 2, Malibu, 25-50.

Van der Meijden, H. 1993
Terrakotta-arulae aus Sizilien und Unteritalien, Amsterdam.

Viola, L. 1881
Taranto, Notizie degli Scavi di Antichità 1881, 376-436.

Viola, L. 1883
Taranto, Notizie degli Scavi di Antichità, 178-189.

Viola, L. 1888
Taranto, Notizie degli Scavi di Antichità, 751-752.

Wuilleumier, P. 1939
Tarente: des origins à la conquête romaine, Paris.

Notes

1. This article was written while an Enbom Visiting Scholar at the National Museum of Antiquities in Copenhagen in November 2009 and reworked in 2014. I am very grateful to Dr Bodil Bundgaard Rasmussen for her kindness and hospitality during my stay. On Tarentine terracottas see Wuilleumier 1939, 393-439; Herdejürgen 1971 and 1978; Kingsley 1976; Lippolis et al. 1995; see also Poli 2010 and Bencze 2013.

2. An early group ended up in the Copenhagen National Museum: Breitenstein 1941, vii – they had been acquired by Prince Christian Frederick in 1820 when he purchased the collection of Giuseppe Capecelatro, Archbishop of Taranto. See further Lippolis et al. 1995, 73, "g.2 stipe" of the Fondo Giovinazzi; on p. 42, he assigns as a date of discovery the year 1790. Note also a collection made in 1771 from the same area: Carducci 1771; Lippolis et al. 1995, 73 "g.1 stipe".

3. Fondo Giovinazzi: Viola 1881, 408; Lenormant 1881-1882, 148-90; Lenormant 1882, 202-5; Evans 1886, 8-23; Wuilleumier 1939, 399-404 (pl. 29, 1 is a mould); Lippolis et al. 1995, 73-4 (g.3).

4. Fondo Pizzone: Viola 1883, 184-185; Evans 1886, 23-31; Wuilleumier 1939, 396-398; Lippolis et al. 1995, 78, (g.1)

5. See in general Lippolis et al. 1995.

6. Copenhagen, NM inv. no. 3352: Breitenstein 1941, 46 no. 409, pl. 50 (ht. 11.4 cms). London, BM, GR 1888,1212.17: Higgins 1954, no. 1360 (made up of two joining frr.; thickness 1.0-2.5 cm).

7. Letters of Helbig, Copenhagen National Museum. On Helbig, see Moltesen 1987, 42-43; and Moltesen 2012.

8. Copenhagen, NM inv. nos. 3334-3352: Breitenstein 1941, 45-46, nos. 399-417.

9. The sale was channelled through A. van Branteghem, letters in the Greek and Roman Department, British Museum.

10. Cf. Breitenstein 1941, 45, who describes the Copenhagen material as a "collective find of moulds".

11. Viola 1888, 751-2; Lippolis et al. 1995, 91-92 and 94 (B. 3, g.2 = Viola report) with 181 -182, pls. 50-56.

12. On Tarentine moulds see Wuilleumier 1939, 394-395; Kingsley 1981, 41-58.

13. Cf. London, BM GR 1888.12-12.3, a mould fragment with similar fruit, but an olive or myrtle wreath.

14. Bennett et al. 2002, 150-1 no. 12. On the findspot see further, Lippolis et al. 1996, 57 and 63 (fig.); and see 74 no. 67, cf. also 73 no. 63 and 75 no. 70 (A. Dell'Aglio).

15. Neutsch 1967, 128-129 and 172-173, pl. 27, 2 (width 18.5) with pl. 27, 1.

16. For an antefix mould with rounded contour, cf. Neutsch 1967, 164, pl. 22, 2-3 no. X.1 (ht. 20.4).

17. For other votive plaques see Wuilleumier 1939, 429-432.

18. Wuilleumier 1939, 432-6, pls. 41-2, especially 42, 2 (width c. 18 cms). For the scene cf. also van der Meijden 1993 pl. 53 (MW 7). The mould fragment, Copenhagen, NM inv. no. 3351 (Breitenstein 1941, no. 408), seems to have the frontal head of a tiny figure in a similar position.

19. On altars see most recently, van der Meijden 1993 and Lentini (ed.) 1993. For moulds for altars see van der Meijden 1993, 348 (MA 3), pl. 57 – bride on *kline*; and 348 (MA 4) – head surrounded by scrolls (for the type see van der Meijden 1993, pl. 52 MW 1).

20. Getty 86.AD.598.1 and 2: Salapata 2001, 25-50.

21. Lippolis et al. 1995, 202-3, pl. 57, 3. On such cults cf. further Hinz 1998, 144-152.

22. Evans 1886, 12 with 22 no. 22, notes an ivy canopy around the figure of the woman seated on the end of the couch on one of the examples of this type, the complex iconography of which remains a puzzle. Moulds for bearded heads of reclining figures are to be found among the British Museum group (London, BM GR 1888,1212.7 and 22). For some of the complexities of understanding such figures see Kingsley 1979, 201-20; Lippolis 2001, 225-255; Lippolis 2005, 91-102. For connections

between Demeter and Dio-
nysos cults, and their mysteries
see Burkert 1987 5, 77-78 and
Burkert 1985, 285-301.

23. Copenhagen, NM inv.nos.
3337-9 and 3345: Breitenstein
1941 nos. 412-415.

24. London, BM GR
1888,1212.10-11 and 13 (E
34-35 and 14).

25. On the uses of the Tarentine examples see also van der Meijden
1993, 153-183. On thymiateria
in general see most recently
Massar 2008.

Fig. 1.
Fragments of a funerary plaque. Acquired in Athens 1863 by Cosmus Bræstrup and Jean Pio. Collection of Classical and Near Eastern Antiquities, National Museum of Denmark. Photo John Lee, National Museum of Denmark.

responsible for the reform that laid the foundation for the modern Danish police force. Bræstrup spoke several languages, among them modern Greek, and this, in combination with his legal skills, made him particularly eligible as a member of the diplomatic mission to Athens in 1863 at the time when the Danish Prince Vilhelm was made King Georg 1st. His stay in Athens was brief, but he probably accompanied the young King to Korfu in June 1864 for the ceremonial hand over of the Ionian Islands. Later in 1864 he was dispatched on another diplomatic mission this time to Berlin.[6]

JEAN PIO

Jean Pio (1833-84), fig. 3[7] graduated from the University of Copenhagen in 1857 in history and philology having also acquired an excellent knowledge of Modern Greek. Awaiting a chair at a university in Modern Greek, he took up a teaching position in "Borgerdydskolen"[8]. In the end, the university chair in Modern Greek did not open up and Pio continued his career in teaching, first as a private teacher and from 1868 as head of "Borgerdydskolen". The school thrived under his leadership as a result of his genuine interest in education. He was much influenced by John Amos Comenius (1592-1670), the father of modern education, and translated his major work *Didactica Magna* into Danish. Pio published several books related to French, Modern Greek, and Danish as well as translations and many papers for educational periodicals, even establishing one himself.[9]

is, of course, compressed into one scene and focuses on the *prothesis* only, the lay-
ing out of the dead in the house or in the porch and the mourning around the
bier, a moment that served both key emotional and practical functions – it gave
the family a last chance to see the deceased and to mourn, but it also served to
certify death and to formalize the transfer of property or other inheritance. The
shape has been modified to include a small projecting ledge above. This suggests
the possibility that they were not attached to a complete, house-like structure,
in the manner of the Exekias series, but perhaps rather to a retaining wall behind which were several burials. The projection might well imitate the eaves
that protected the series of plaques somewhat when attached to the mud-brick
structures.[30] The sequence of singletons begins after the multiple series, running
from about 530/20 BC down to about 490 BC, or soon after.[31] Boardman linked
the reduction from elaborate series to single *pinax* with a possible restriction on
grave decoration, with Peisistratos reinforcing Solon's changes, perhaps as a result
of his own political need to control the aristocracy.[32] It is tempting to link the
final abandonment in the period 490/80 with further social changes following
the Persian Wars and the sacking of the city.

*Fig. 6.
Phormiskos with prothesis
scene. After Archäologischer
Anzeiger 1935, 298,
Abb. 24.*

THE COPENHAGEN PINAX

The Copenhagen *pinax*, which was a late singleton, is sadly very fragmentary and the full extent of the scene cannot be made out with any certainty, but there are some interesting details. The scene was clearly the *prothesis* of a young man, surrounded by mourning figures, fig. 7. It is the day after the death and his body has been bathed and anointed with sweet smelling oil. He has been laid on the bier, bed or couch, his body wrapped in a tight shroud (*endyma*) and his head propped against a cushion and adorned with flowers. The large pair of joining fragments tells us most, for here we find the top of the head and the brow of the deceased male, encircled by a red garland with large blossoms and resting on a folded cushion. To the left is the brow of a woman bent low over the corpse. She has one hand up to the top of her own head, striking it or pressing against it, the other is to be seen under the deceased's head, between it and the cushion.[33] She is in deep mourning and would seem to be giving the deceased a last embrace.[34] From other scenes on *pinakes*, and on vases, we can identify her as the deceased's mother (so labeled *meter* on the Sappho Painter's plaque in the Louvre),[35] while her action is immortalized in Homer's *Iliad* (24, 723-4) – "and among them white-armed Andromache led the lament, holding the head of man-slaying Hektor in her arms ..."

To the right, a second woman bends over the deceased's head. Her hair is loose and disheveled, her left hand to her brow, her right disappears behind her head with three fingers appearing fanned vertically. She wears a necklace (represented by a wavy line), a *chiton* and a wrap around her neck and shoulders. This position behind the head of the bier and the stooping pose seem to be associated with the grandmother.[36] On the Louvre plaque by the Sappho Painter she is, indeed, labeled *thethe* (for *tethe*).[37]

In the background behind these two women, the mother and grandmother, are the remains of a third woman. Her head and body were facing to the left – we see the long strands of her hair over her white neck, a double necklace (wavy line and straight line), and part of her left forearm raised in mourning over the head of the stooping figure. She wore a wrap, part of which can be made out between her and her companion's face. She might be thought to be the man's wife, if he was already married. The presence of the deceased's spouse is not noted on the Sappho Painter's pinax, where the deceased may have been an unmarried girl.

A loose fragment provides part of a fourth female mourner, fig. 8. She faces to the right and must have been one of the mourners further down the bier, flanking it. She has loose hair, a necklace (wavy line) and wears a *chiton* and a wrap about her shoulders and over her upper arms. Both arms seem to have been raised in the ritual gesture of mourning. Such additional mourning women near the bier

are to be thought of as close relatives, aunts, as on the plaque by the Sappho Painter in the Louvre where they are labeled *thethis* and even *thethis prospatros*, or sisters,[38] although these are usually shown as being considerably younger than the deceased.[39] The deliberate concentration on such close family connections recall the legislation brought in by Solon at the beginning of the sixth century which sought to limit extravagant display at funerals.[40]

An important fragment from the upper right-hand corner of the plaque may be taken with remains of drapery to the right of the group of women at the deceased's head, see fig. 7. The drapery, a large cloak or himation, indicates that the figure faced to the right, away from the women and the bier, and that the right forearm was horizontal. This unattached fragment, fig. 9, has part of the head of a figure with white hair, who has put his right hand up to his head. We see his straight thumb and his four bent fingers, their tips protruding to the left of the thumb – that it is a man is clear from the absence of added white on the hand. He has buried his hand in his white hair, clumps of which appear between fingers and thumb. The old man, no doubt the deceased's grandfather, has turned away in deep pain, his hand to his head, his upper body and head bent low as he mourns the loss of his grandson.[41] If no man should bury his own son, then how much more is that true of a grandfather and his grandson? This highly evocative figure is a new addition to the most intimate circle of the mourners. In other representations of the *prothesis* a white haired man is to be found among the group of men approaching the bier from the left, arms extended – he may have been intended to be the grandfather, or perhaps rather an elderly uncle or other revered relative.[42]

Fig. 9.
Fragment from the upper right corner of the plaque showing a whitehaired man in mourning.

This fragment also has the turn from the vertical border on the right (a line and a wide band that is framed on either side by a strongly painted edging line) into the horizontal band above the scene and also reveals the beginning of the jutting ledge on the top of the plaque. Two other fragments give us part of this upper edge. One has, on the facing edge of the eave, the remains of a simple gear-like pattern made up of interlocking thick vertical lines of which only the bounding edges are preserved, fig. 10. The other comes from the top left corner of the plaque, but the jutting eave has broken away, fig. 11. None of the fragments preserve fixing holes for the plaque. The right hand edge of the plaque, however, has been decorated with a simple pattern of widely spaced and roughly formed squares, so that it is clear that the plaque was not set into any plaster mount, but hung free.

The remaining fragments of the Copenhagen plaque are not easy to interpret but all have parts of the drapery of the figures gathered around the bier. One has in addition to large, boldly done stacked pleats, two horizontal bands – the upper one plain, the lower carrying a cross-hatched panel, fig. 12. This must be part of the deceased's shroud with below it a section of the mattress on which he has been laid.[43]

The iconography of death and burial has been much studied in recent years, especially by Alan Shapiro and John Oakley.[44] The elements to be discerned on the fragmentary Copenhagen plaque follow the expected pattern, apart from the action of the old man at the extreme right of the scene. The inclusion among the mourning women near the head of the bier of such an elderly mourning man seems to be a feature of fifth-century *prothesis* scenes, for we find him

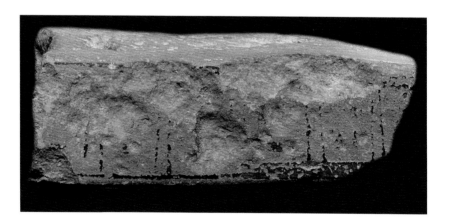

Fig. 10.
Fragment from the top edge of the plaque with the decorated eave.

Fig. 11.
Fragment from the top edge of the plaque, eave broken away.

Fig. 12.
Fragment showing, on the right, part of the shroud and the bier's matress below.

on three of the Sabouroff Painter's white-ground lekythoi[45] and on two red-figured loutrophoroi,[46] all of the second quarter of the fifth century BC. It is perhaps that, following the deaths of so many young men in the Persian Wars, the role of the grandfather as a principle mourner began to be recognized. The Copenhagen plaque is probably to be dated around 490-80 BC, and the only other examples of a man in such a position are on two late black-figure plaques.[47] On these two pieces the arrangement of the figures may be little more than a compositional device: there is certainly nothing of the strong emotional charge that is carried on the Copenhagen plaque, as the old man so poignantly turns away. The appearance of a further old man on one of the so-called Huge Lekythoi would thus also perhaps reflect the heavy casualties of the end of the Peloponnesian War.[48]

The Copenhagen fragments were first associated with the Kleophrades Painter by Rumpf.[49] In his monograph on the Kleophrades Painter, Beazley accepted Rumpf's idea and included them in his list as "these bf. frr. may be by the Kleophrades Painter".[50] Years later Beazley remarked that the fragments were "at least near the Kleophrades Painter".[51] The lining of the lips is very Kleophradean, as is the added wave in the steps of drapery pleats and perhaps the rich curls of hair. It is true, however, that the prominent curl for the nostril is not to be seen, but there is only one well preserved head, and that the ear, although it has the typical strong lobe, does not have all the complex upper curves. The chin of the women mourners may seem rather more pointed than on the Kleophrades Painter's red-figure works, but perhaps the stooping pose has affected the painter's more monumental form. In conclusion, it seems likely that, despite Beazley's hesitation, Rumpf was correct to see this plaque as the work of the Kleophrades Painter. The speed required in producing what might have been a commissioned work could be responsible for the fluidity of the style, but the emotional power of the mourning women, fig. 13, and the old grandfather turned away, fig. 9, are surely the Kleophrades Painter's.

As a coda to this brief paper, we might mention an isolated and unpublished fragment from a funerary plaque in the British Museum.[52] It was given anonymously in 1935, together with two other dubious pieces. Cleaning of the fragment revealed that it was not, however, a fake, but had been ingeniously reworked. Some of the black slip had been carefully scraped away, the fragment turned up-side-down and then the remainder re-engraved to show parts of two women, added red and white being further employed to give the whole a more authentic air, fig. 14 left.

Despite this barbarous treatment, we can still make out some of the original design, fig. 14 right.[53] There was clearly the lower part of a female figure to the right. We can make out the ends of her cloak, finely drawn and with a line border,

Fig. 13.
Mourning women gathered
around the head of the
deceased.

Fig. 14.
Fragment of funerary plaque, British Museum GR 1935.5-2.1 fr. Drawing by Kate Morton.

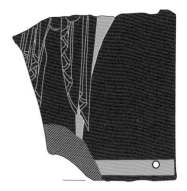

and part of her plain *chiton*, with a scalloped tuck just above her bottom. In the right hand corner is a large black area with a steeply curved edge nearest the woman. This can only really be the edge of a funerary mound. Below the scene was a border, either reserved or with a pattern now completely lost, and in the right hand lower corner a fixing hole. The lower edge and the right edge of the plaque are both painted with added red.

The drapery, especially the scalloped tuck recalls the Sappho Painter, while the black-figure loutrophoros in Athens by that vase-painter has, in addition to the regular *prothesis* on one side of the body of the vase and the interment on the other, a representation of the mound on the neck.[54] The Sappho Painter was clearly something of a specialist in black-figure representations of funerary scenes and it would be quite easy to see this ruined fragment as one of his works, a work which uniquely, it would seem, included the mound on a funerary plaque.

ACKNOWLEDGEMENTS

The authors would like to thank David Saunders, J. Paul Getty Museum for the image of the Getty fragment of a plaque and Kate Morton at the British Museum for her drawings of the British Museum fragment, fake and original.

Fig. 1.
Side A. After A. Scotti,
Illustrazione de un vaso
italo-greco del museo de
Monsignor Arcivescovo
di Taranto, pl. 1. Napoli
1811.

crested Corinthian helmets and one carries a round shield emblazoned with a kantharos. As for the inscriptions, we find between the woman and the horses ΕΡΙΦΥΛΕ, placed vertically, and slanting from the hores's legs to the woman's feet ΚΑΛΙΦΟΡΑ. Above the horse, on the right side of the chariot, arranged horizontally and retrograde, we find ΑΡΙΣΤΟΣ.

The composition on side B is almost identical, fig. 2. A woman stands in front of a chariot wrapped quite tightly in a cloak which falls down her back. With her left hand she lifts up the hem of the cloak. The chariot here is also drawn by four horses. Of the two men in the chariot one is a charioteer or a hoplite wearing an open-faced Attic helmet and the other a hoplite wearing a crested Corinthian helmet and carrying a shield with a left leg as an emblem. The inscriptions are, in front of the woman written vertically, ΚΑΛΟΠΑ and between the men in the chariot and the horses' heads written horizontally and retrograde, ΑΜΦΙΑΡΑΟΣ.

The inscriptions made Abbot Scotti interpret the scenes as belonging to the myth of "The Seven against Thebes", the story of Polyneikes and his followers waging war against his brother Eteokles in Thebes. Both scenes illustrating the moment where Eriphyle takes leave of her husband Amphiaraos, the brother in law of king Adrastos of Argos. Amphiaraos, being also a seer, had refused to join the expedition as he could predict that all but Adrastos would perish in the future battle. Polyneikes makes Eriphyle persuade her husband to join the expedition by presenting her with a beautiful necklace, given by the goddess Aphrodite to his

Fig. 2.
Side B. After A. Scotti,
Illustrazione de un vaso
italo-greco del museo de
Monsignor Arcivescovo
di Taranto, pl. 2. Napoli
1811.

great-great-great-grandmother Harmonia. Being unaware of the consequences, Eriphyle duly persuades Amphiaraos to join the expedition – with the disastrous result that he had foreseen.

Scotti concluded that the vase was Greek but made in Sicily in the period 700-550 BC.[5] Furthermore he took it for a gift to a victorious athlete.[6]

THE ANTIQUARIAN DEBATE

Abbot Scotti's publication, 116 pages with extensive notes, created quite a stir and was followed by several attacks and counterattacks from other Neapolitan scholars. The Abbot Pasquale Ponticelli in 1813 published a very negative review, claiming that Scotti's translations of the ancient literature had many flaws and that he had misunderstood the inscriptions.[7]

Such criticisms required a defense of Scotti, which duly came in the form of a published letter to Capece Latro from the nom de plume, Crestofili Parresiaste[8]. Here, in turn, Ponticelli's work on the inscriptions was ridiculed. In 1814 this was followed by another letter from a nom de plume, Filalete, to someone named Critobulo, figs. 3-4.[9] This letter dealt with Parresiaste's work in defence of Scotti. It was extremely ironic when describing the career of Abbot Scotti – a theologian, he claimed, who by publishing a work on something he had no knowledge about suddenly for no reason became well known. The letter was also very harsh towards Scotti's defender Crestofili Parresiaste. This debate might

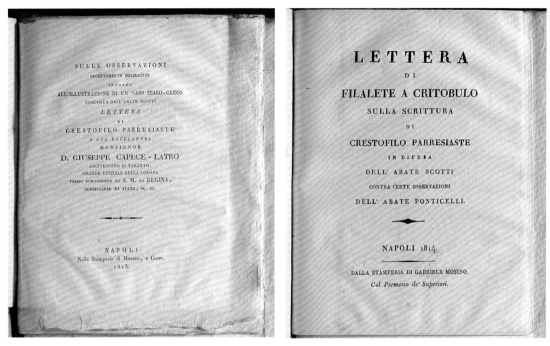

Fig. 3-4.
Frontispieces of the two letters by nom de plumes, Lettera di Crestofilo Parresiaste and Lettera di Filalete. Classical and Near Eastern Antiquities, National Museum of Denmark.

have continued had it not been for the political situation in Naples which gave even the scholars and antiquarians something else to think about.[10]

THE FIRST SCHOLARLY PUBLICATION

While this was going on the amphora was published in 1813 by J.V. Millingen in his "Peintures antiques et inedites de vases grecs tirées de divers collections, avec des explication".[11] Millingen divided the vases into seven groups: 1.Divinités; 2. Heroïques; 3. Dionysiaques; 4.Vie civile; 5.Cérémonies funèbres; 6. Gymnases; 7. Mystères. Naturally he placed the amphora in question in the second group – Heroïques. He was, like Scotti, particularly interested in the inscriptions: "Les vases avec les inscriptions sont particulièrement interessans ..."[12] He believed that the amphora belonged in an era in which the art of drawing still was in need of inscriptions in order to identify the figures in the scenes.

   Millingen, however, approached the study of vases with more caution than the antiquarians who had taken part in the debate aroused by Scotti's publication. Although he too stressed the importance of inscriptions he also treated the vases as archaeological objects of great interest and was acutely aware that they were perhaps not always quite as they seemed. Thus he put in his introduction the following assurance: "Aussi, dans ce recueil, on ne publie que des vases sains, ou ceux restaurés que l'on a vus et examinés avec le plus grand soins". On a technical note, he continued that "Heureusement que l'imposture se découvre plus facilement dans cette branche de l'antiquité, que dans toute autre; en frottant les vases ou on en soupçonnne avec une éponge tempée dans l'eau forte ou de l'esprit de vin rectifié, on fait disparoître tous les repeints".[13]

With this statement Millingen demonstrated his awareness of the dangers to which the scholars and antiquarians were exposed by restorers. In addition he also disclosed a knowledge about those restorers as revealed by the following statement: "Plusieurs artistes surtout à Naples, ont porté l'art de restaurer les vases au plus haut degree de perfection. On peut même dire à une perfection dangereuse pour la science, d'apres la difficulté qui en résulte de distinguer les parties restaurées".[14] Even with this awareness and knowledge Millingen in his publication did not mention any restorations when describing the vases – presumably because he did not, after all, detect any.

A DANISH PRINCE IN NAPLES

This story begins in 1818 when the Danish Prince Christian Frederik and his wife Caroline Amalie left Denmark on a grand tour of Europe, fig. 5. In December of 1819 they arrived in Rome. There they were met and entertained by the Danish classicist P. O. Brøndsted, who in 1818 had been appointed 'agent of the Royal Danish Court to the Holy See'.[15] Already in January 1820 the royal couple travelled on to Naples. Here the couple were received by King Ferdinand of the Two Sicilies and they quickly became part of the social life of Naples which seems to have been very lively according to the Prince's diaries of which he kept two, a calendar in Danish and a travel diary in French.[16]

As a boy, Prince Christian Frederik had already proved a keen collector of coins and minerals and, when at the age of 16 he was introduced to Classical Antiquity by his tutor, he made a promise to himself in his diary, "I must also improve my knowledge of Roman and Greek History". Thus, thanks to his tutor and his own inclinations he arrived well prepared in Naples.[17]

The Prince immediately went off in pursuit of his various interests – making the acquaintance of the renowned mineralogist Abbot Teodore Monticelli, visiting the Archaeological Museum, and attending meetings in various scientific societies. In "Società Reale Borbonnica-Accademia Reale delle Scienzee" he was later, on March 17th 1820, to give a lecture on Vesuvius.[18]

Fig. 5.
Prince Christian Frederik
and Princess Caroline
Amalie. Drawing by
Bertel Thorvaldsen 1820.
Hirschsprung Collection,
Copenhagen.

Teodore Monticelli introduced the Prince to the former archbishop of Tarento Giuseppe Capece Latro, fig. 7,[19] and already on the 19th of January the Royal couple paid a visit to the archbishop. "Ce matin j'eus le plaisir de faire la connaissance de l'ancien Archevêque de Tarente, le grand ami de mad. Brun, qui me recut avec affection la plus marquée et qui s'empressa de me montrer les tableaux dont ses appartemens sont ornés, mais particulièrement la belle vue de ses fenêtres. La maison est située sur la hauteur de Pizzofalcone, et elle est la même qu'habitait Lady Hamilton nombre d'années".[20]

Madame Brun (1765-1835) mentioned by the Prince,[21] was the sister of the learned bishop of Copenhagen Frederik Münter (1761-1830), who had travelled widely and was well acquainted with intellectuals and antiquarians throughout Europe.[22] In 1785 and 1786 he visited Naples and met several of the vase collectors in and around Naples.[23] In a letter to her brother she characterized him as "einer der schönsten Geiseköpfe, die je ein antiker Marmor verewigt hätte".[24]

The day of this memorable meeting, 19th January 1820, also left the Prince time for a visit to the Archaeological Museum. The Prince was captivated by the vases and writes in his French diary, "On connaît parfaitement l'art de restaurer ces vases lorsqu'on les trouvent brisées et on les imite aussi en grande perfection pour tromper les étrangers, mais la prevue certain c'est que la peinture sur les moderns ne résiste pas a l'acide et souvent pas meme à l'eau tandis que la peinture antique est indestructible."[25]

The royal couple made several visits to Capece Latro and one of these took them to his country house at Portici south of Naples, where the Prince for the

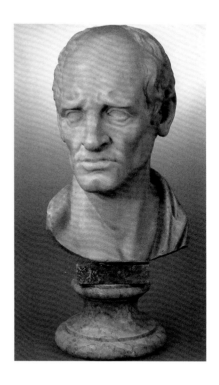

Fig. 6.
Archbishop Giuseppe Capece Latro
(1744-1836). Portrait by C.D. Rauch 1810.
National Museum of Denmark. Classical and
Near Eastern Antiquities, National Museum of
Denmark.

first time became aware of the Archbishop's collection of Antiquities – noting in particular the vases: "Cette campagne est un vrai bijou, bien situé et commodément arrangée ... quelle vue de la terasse sur tout le Golfe et sur Naples! Elle renferme sa collection de vases et d'antiquités, don't il a fait lui même la description, il y a bien une trentaine de vases parmi lesquelles de fort belles avec des peintures grecs – ou étrusque comme on l'appelle – quelquesunes avec des caractères ... L'aimable hôte trouvais tant de plaisir à nous montrer ce charmant Casino. Son buste travaillé par Rauch et qui appartient à madame Brun se trouve là, en attendant l'occasion de l'envoyer en Dannemark.[26] The bust never reached Madame Brun but remained with the collection in the royal palace where the sculptor himself, Christian Daniel Rauch, saw it during a visit to the King in 1845, fig. 5.[27]

During further visits the Prince developed an interest in Capece Latro's collection of antiquities and the archbishop was keen to further this interest, as he wanted to sell his collection. However, nothing came of this as the Prince had to leave Naples in March to return to his royal duties in Denmark. He was, however, not keen to go back home and asked permission from the King to prolong his stay. This was duly granted and the royal couple, who had remained in Rome as the Prince fell ill, returned to Naples in May.

THE ACQUISITION OF GIUSEPPE CAPECE LATRO'S COLLECTION

Friendships were soon renewed and negotiations about a possible acquisition of the archbishop's collection were reopened. Capece Latro suggested that the Prince acquired it on the basis of paying him an annuity of 200 Neapolitan ducats a month for the rest of his life. Being tempted the Prince asked P. O. Brøndsted to join him in Naples and make an evaluation of the collection. Brøndsted embarked on the task immediately. Apart from studying the vases he had at his disposal two catalogues, one of 123 objects which he mentions in his report and another of 13 of the most interesting vases in the collection.[28] In the latter catalogue the Amphiaraos amphora is no. three and the description includes a reference to Abbott Scotti's publication. After about three weeks Brøndsted handed over his evaluation:[29]

"Your Highness
Prince Christian Frederik of Denmark

Gracious Lord!
As Your Highness's commanded I went yesterday to Portici and examined with care the Vase Collection of Monsignore Capece-Latro, and I now have the Honour of presenting my Opinion of the same:

Among the 123 items to which the brief Catalogue displayed in the Collection corresponds, are to be found 15 or 16 Pieces which may be reckoned in every collection as of the first Importance Of these 16 there is one which in antiquarian and art-historical respects will be assigned by all knowledgeable people a Rank in the first Class, of that kind of Monument, and two others which are also superbly beautiful and of which I believe that a closer Study of the Scenes will also move me to reckon in the first Class.

The one most excellent is the Sicilian Greek Vase with black Figures in the oldest Style on yellow Ground, the Scenes depicted of which are taken from the Myth of Amphiaros and Eriphyle and which Messrs Scotti and Millingen have elucidated. Among this Vase's other interesting qualities there is the significant that it is one of the very smallest and also best restored, regardless of the fact that it must have been broken in many pieces …

Among the others are only very few which could prompt me to devote a significant Space of Time on the interpretation of the Scenes depicted. Among these few is, in particular, the great Vase which corresponds to No. 3 in the

Fig. 7.
The most excellent Sicilian Greek
Vase. Side A.

Catalogue and which has curious Scenes depicted. Mnsr Capece Latro, himself, in a Manuscript of which I have been informed, attempted to interpret this, but in every way erroneously. All in all Monsignore's interpretation of the depicted Scenes, which he has taken upon himself to attempt, is a quaint Example of how even an Admirable Prelate with superficial insight into the nature of Hellenic Antiquity, can attribute to this brilliant Race's not always decent artists all manner of beautiful and Christian Sentiments as those Rogues never dreamt of.

What in particular would frighten me from scholarly Preoccupation with most of the larger vases of this Collection, is the already formerly-conceived and now even further strengthened Opinion as to the vigorous Restoration which most of the pieces have had to suffer: this I expressed already in my previous letter to Your ryl: Highness.

Restoration is taken so far on many Vases that if not whole then often half-figures with their Attributes, Movement and other Circumstances, which furnish the Motifs of the Action are inserted into the scenes on the Surface of the Vase. Once one notices that, then for everybody who wishes to know what an ancient Greek artist in the condition of the motifs of his Genius, his own Religion, Belief, History and Nationality thought and wrought and not what some modern Peter or Paul, in a Study of Restoration, working in a some fairly arbitrary, un-antique and un-artistic Routine, or at his own Convenience, has put together, the desire to interpret simply fades away …

The pecuniary Value of this Collection is difficult for me to determine, particularly as I, not to communicate to Yr: ryl: Highness another Opinion than my own in this Matter, have not wished to consult any of the many here so-called Antiquarians, who have, much more than I, occupied themselves with buying and selling of this Kind of Memorial.

However, I do believe, after Consideration of the Prices I frequently remarked both in Paris, here in Italy and in Greece, that I would not be far wrong if I estimate the Worth of the Collection at 20,000 ducats. That this Collection would be a true prize for Denmark speaks for itself. But how much Annuity one could, on Acquisition of the aforementioned, bestow upon a kind and worthy Gentleman of advanced Years, I dare not reckon; also I must confess that, in a sense, my feelings recoil from considering how much longer we could reasonably hope to have our dear Archbishop of Taranto among us."

In his report Brøndsted demonstrates awareness of the heavy restoration of many of the vases in the collection. He does not, however, express any reservations regarding the black-figure amphora. This early in the 19th century Classical antiquities had not yet reached Denmark in any significant number[30] and Brøndsted saw here an opportunity to change this state of affairs. Brøndsted's evaluation ended up being 20.000 golden Neapolitan ducats. On his recommendation a group of portraits and an a number of other objects in marble and bronze were added to the collection.[31]

Meanwhile the archbishop asked Andrea de Iorio from the Archaeological Museum "and an artist", Rafaele Gargiulo an artist and renowned restorer of ancient vases,[32] to look through the collection and give an estimate of its value without telling them what he had in mind. Like Brøndsted Andrea de Iorio also considered the Amphiaraos amphora the star of the collection setting its value at 3000 piastre[33], figs.7-8, which is quite understandable as the vase had already been the object of much interest arising from Scotti's publication. The Prince then suggested to Capece Latro a lifelong monthly payment of 150 ducats to which he agreed. The archbishop was at the time 77 years old and lived to be 92, so the final price ended well above 20.000 ducats. The Prince and the archbishop

Fig. 8.
The most excellent Sicilian Greek
Vase. Side B.

remained friends and kept up a correspondence right up until the time of Capece Latro's death in 1836.[34]

A VASE CABINET IS BORN

The collection acquired in Naples did not reach Copenhagen until 1825,[35] when the Prince created his Vase Cabinet at the royal palace, Amalienborg – the first collection of Greek and South Italian vases in Denmark. The Prince spent a lot of time in the Cabinet in the 1820s and 1830s and was much involved in the acquisitions made. He had valuable help from professor P. O. Brøndsted who had assisted the Prince in Naples and the diplomat/archaeologist Christian Tuxen Falbe, whom he had invited to work on the collection. When the Prince in 1839 succeeded his cousin as king of Denmark he, of course, had less time on his hands and acquisitions were more or less left to Brøndsted[36] and Falbe.[37] The collection grew steadily with vases presented to the Prince by Brøndsted and

Fig. 9.
P. O. Brøndsted (1780-1842) C. A. Jensen 1827. Ny Carlsberg Glyptotek. Copenhagen.

Fig. 10.
C. T. Falbe (1791-1948). Contemporary copy of a miniature
portrait by L. Fraenkel 1815, Private collection.

Falbe or acquisitions made at auctions in Europe.[38] In 1847 Falbe acquired the
collection formed by the Danish Architect Christian Hansen during his 16 year
stay in Athens for the Vase Cabinet[39]. The same year the King asked J. L. Ussing,
professor of philology and archaeology at the University of Copenhagen, to publish the most interesting vases in the collection. Ussing commissioned drawings to
be made by several Danish artists, but the King died in 1848 and the publication
was never finished, so we have no knowledge of whether the amphora would
have been included.[40] After the King's death his collection became state property
and to this day forms the core of the Collection of Classical and Near Eastern
Antiquities at the National Museum of Denmark.[41]

Fig. 12.
The Amphiaraosamphora
after conservation. Side B.

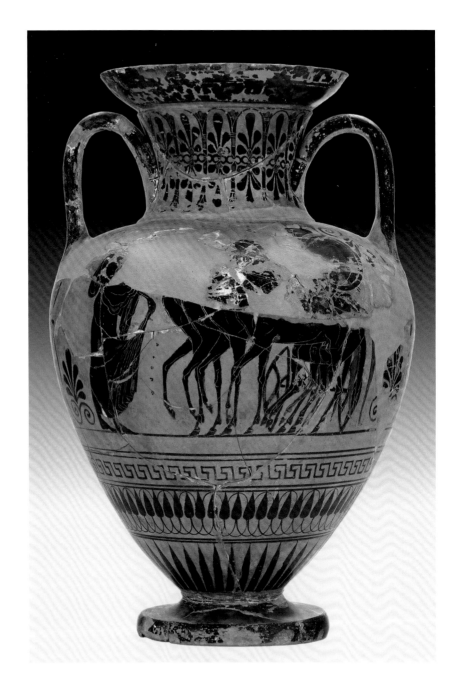

Bibliography

Beazley, J. D.
Some Inscriptions on Vases, V,
American Journal of Archaeology,
1950, 315, 6.

Beazley, J.D. 1956/1978
Attic Black-figure Vase-painters,
Oxford/New York,

Birket Smith, S. 1862
De malede vaser i Antikcabinettet,
København.

Bobé, L. 1910
Frederikke Brun født Münter og
hendes Kreds, hjemme og ude,
København.

Brun, F. 1818
Episoden IV. Sitten udn
Landschaftstudien von Neapel und
seine Umgebungen in Briefen
and Zuschriften entworfen in den
Jahren 1809-1810 nebst späteren
Zusätzen von Frederike Brun
geboren Münter, Leipzig.

Breitenstein, N. 1951
Christian VIII's Vasecabinet, in:
Antikcabinettet 1851. Udgivet i
hundredaaret af Nationalmuseet.
København, 57-176.

Christian 1820
Osservazioni sulla lava del Vesuvio
del 26. Gennajo 1820. Naples,
Nella Stamperia dell'Accademia di
marina, Napoli.

CVA
Corpus Vasorum Antiquorum,
Denmark fasc. 3, Copenhagen.

Dagbøger II, 1
Fabritius, A. et al. Kong Christian
VIIIs Dagbøger og Optegnelser
udgivet af Det Kongelige Selskab til
Fædrelandets Historie, København
1973.

Eggers, F. & K. 1873-1891
Christian Daniel Rauch, Vol. 1-5,
Berlin.

Filalete 1814
Lettera di Filalete a Critobulo sulla
scrittura di Crestofilo Parresiaste,
Napoli.

Fischer-Hansen, T. 2010
Frederik Münter og hans rejse
til Italien – med særligt henblik
på hans erfaringer fra Sicilien.
(Frederik Münter and his sojourn
in Italy with special reagard to
Sicily). Aarbøger for nordisk
Oldkyndighed og Historie/Annual
og the Royal Society of Northern

Antiquaries 2007, Copenhagen,
91-106.

Gundestrup, B. 199
The Royal Danish Kunstkammer
1737. I-II + Index, Copenhagen.

Haugsted, I. 1996
Dream and Reality. Danish
antiquaries, architects and artists in
Greece, London.

Interpretazione, no year
Di alcuni Vasi Etruschi esistenti
nella collezione di sua Eccelenza
Monsignor Guiuaeppe Capece
Latro, Patrizio Napoletano antico.
Arcivescovo di Taranto.

Jenkins, I. & Sloan, K., 1996
Vases and Volcanoes. Sir william
Hamilton and his Collection,
London.

Lund, J. 2000
Royal connoisseur and consular
collector: the part played by C. T.
Falbe in collecting antiquities from
Tunisia, Greece and Rome for
Christian VIII, in: Rasmussen, B. B.
et al. (eds.), Christian VIII and the
National Museum. Antiquities –
Coins – Medals, Copenhagen,
119-149.

Lyons, C. 1992
The Museo Mastrilli and the Culture of Collecting in Naples, 1700-1755. Journal of the History of Collections 4, no. 2, 1-26.

Madsen,O.
Christian VIII.s sygdom og død. Danske Magazin, series 9, vol. 1, part 1, København, 72-96.

Masci, E.
The birth of ancient vase collecting in Naples in the early eighteenth century. Antiquarian studies, excavations and collections. Journal of the History of Collections, 2007, vol. 19 no. 11 pp. 215-224.

Melander, T. 1984
Thorvaldsens græske vaser, København.

Melander, T. 2000
Corpus Vasorum Antiquorum, Thorvaldsens Museum fasc. 1, Denmark fasc. 9, Copenhagen.

Milanese, A. 2007
Pour ne pas choquer l'oeil. Raffaele Gargiulo e il restauro di vase antichi nel Real Museo di Napoli: opzioni di metodo e oscillazioni di gusto tra 1810 e 1840, in: D'Alconzo, P. (ed.) Glio uomini e le cose I. Figure di restauro e casi di restauro in Italia tra XVIII e XX secolo, Napoli, 18-20.

Milanese, A. 2014
In partenza dal regno. Esportazioni e commercio d'arte e d'antichità a Napoli nella prima metà dell'Ottocento. Le Voci del Museo 31, Firenze.

Millingen, M. 1813
Peintures antiques et inedités de vases grecs: tirées de diverses collections avec des explications, Rome.

Møller, A. M. 2000
What the collections meant to Christian VIII, in: Rasmussen, B. B. et al. (eds.), Christian VIII and the National Museum. Antiquities – Coins – Medals, Copenhagen, 79-99.

Nielsen, M. 2010
Frederik Münter of brødrene Vivenzio i Nola – vaser, kontekster og lag. Aarbøger for nordisk Oldkyndighed og Historie / Annual og the Royal Society of Northern Antiquaries 2007, Copenhagen, 107-148.

Papanicolaou-Christensen, A. 1994
Christian Hansen. Breve og tegninger fra Grækenland, København.

Parresiaste 1813
Lettera di Crestofilo Parresiaste … Simboli che si veggono negli scudi di Adrasto e di Anfiarao. Spiegati ed illustrate dall'Abate Pasquale Ponticelli, Napoli.

Ponticelli 1813
Osservazioni dell'abate Pasquale Pontiocelli sul 'illustrazione di un vaso italo-greco del museum di Monsignore Arcivescono di Taranto composta dall'Abate Scottti, Napoli.

Rasmussen, B. B. & Lund, J. 2004
On the creation of the collection of Classical and Near Eastern Antiquities in the Danish National Museum. Pharos. Journal of the Netherlands Institute in Athens. Volume X (2002), 169-178.

Rasmussen, B. B. 2000
A Danish Prince in Naples, in: Rasmussen, B. B. et al. (eds.), Cristian VIII and the National Museum. Antiquities – Coins – Medals. Copenhagen, 11-43.

Rasmussen, B. B. 2006
De herlige græske vaser. P.O. Brøndsted og Christian VIII's vasekabinet, Nationalmuseets Arbejdsmark. København, 201-221.

Rasmussen,B. B. 2008
"London…in reality the capital of Europe". P. O. Brøndsted's dealings with the British Museum, in: Rasmussen, B. B. et al. (eds.), Peter Oluf Brøndsted (1780-1842). A Danish Classicist in his European Ccontext. Historisk-filosofiske skrifter 31. The Royal Danish Academy of Sciences and Letters, Copenhagen, 143-161.

Saunders, D. & Svoboda, M. 2012
Looking at Apulian Vases in a New Light. http://blogs.getty.edu/iris/looking-at-apulian-vases-in-a-new-light/

Schepelern, O.C. 2008
P. O. Brøndsted as Royal Danish Court Agent in Rome, in Rasmussen, B. B. et al. (eds.), Peter Oluf Brøndsted (1780-1842). A Danish Classicist in his European Context. Historisk-filosofiske skrifter 31. The Royal Danish Academy of Sciences and Letters, Copenhagen, 97-107.

Scotti, A. A. 1813
Illustrazione de un vaso italo-grecio del museo de Monsignor Arcivescovo di Taranto, Napoli.

Slej, K. 1995
Kronprins Frederik som antiquar. Christian Frederiks vandringer i det antike Rom 1819-1821 og mødet med to af Roms førende antiquarer, in Andersen, H.D. (eds.) Klassisk arkæologiske studier 2, København, 273-297.

Snow, C.E. 1986
The Affecter Amphora: a case study in the history of Greek vase restoration. The Journal of the Walters Art Gallery, Baltimore, 44, 2-7.

Steiner 2007
Reading Greek Vases, Cambridge, Mass.

Svoboda, M. 2013
Precision and mastery: identifying the work of Raffaele Gargiulo on four Apulian vases, in Brajer, I.(ed.) Conservation in the Nineteenth Century, Copenhagen, 205-218.

Trolle, S. 1980
Stridens vase. Nationalmuseets arbejdsmark. København, 14-24.

Notes

A shorter version of this paper entitled "Un récit édifiant" is published in L'Europe du vase Antique. Collectioneurs, savants, restaurateurs aux XVIIIe siècles, Burgeois, B. & Denoyelle, M. (eds.). I thank Brigitte Burgeois and Martine Denoyelle for the invitation to the colloquium of the same title held in Paris 31 May – 1 June 2011.

1. The National Museum of Denmark, Collection of Classical and Near Eastern Antiquities, inv.nr. ChrVIII 3. CVA, Denmark fasc.6, pl.106,2a-b. ABV 292,5 attributed to the painter Psiax.
2. Masci 2007.
3. Lyons 1992. Jenkins & Sloan 2003.
4. Scotti 1811.
5. Scotti 1811, 92-94.
6. Scotti 1811, 97.
7. Ponticelli 1813.
8. Paresiaste 1813.
9. Filalete 1814.
10. For this short overview of the debate I have benefitted from the work of my late colleague Steffen Trolle 1980.
11. Millingen 1813, no. XX –XXI, p.336-339.
12. Millingen 1813, p.V-VI.
13. Millingen 1813, p.XII.
14. Millingen 1813, p.XII. All quotes from Millingen 1813 are as they appear in the publication.
15. Schepelern 2008.
16. In the Royal Archive, State Archives of Denmark. Rasmussen 2000,7-13.
17. Dagbøger I, 124. For the collections see Møller 2000.
18. Dagbøger II.1. March 17th 1820: […] je prix le courage de lire

en français les notizes que j'avais faits sur ma visite au Vesuv. Later published in the *Atti of the Academia: Socio onorario dell'Academia delle scienze di Napoli*. Letta alle medisima nella seduta del 17.Luglio 1820 ed inserita nel II.vol degli Atti accademici.
19. I warmly thank Maria Toscani, Univerty of Naples for this piece of information.
20. Breitenstein 1951, 62.
21. Bobé 1910. Brun 1818.
22. Fischer- Hansen 2007.
23. Nielsen 2010,110-116.
24. A letter to Bishop Frederik Münter January 1810, see Bobé 1910, 222.
25. Dagbøger II, 1, 19 January 1820.
26. Dagbøger II,1, February 11th.1820.
27. Eggers 1873-1891, vol. 3, 305.
28. The catalogue of 123 object is lost but the smaller one is in the archives of Collection of Classical and Near Eastern Antiquities, the National Museum of Denmark.
29. Letter in the Royal Archive, Rigsarkivet. English translation by Neil Stanford.
30. Gundestrup 1991 lists 15 classical antiquities in the Royal Danish Kunstkammer.

31. Most of the portraits turnerd out to be of recent date but two stood out – two Julio-Claudian princes, inv.no. ChrVIII 305 Germanicus and ChrVIII 303 Drusus.
32. Milanese 2007. Milanese 2014, 201-255.
33. Manuscript in the archives of the National Museum of Denmark, Collection of Classical and Near Eastern Antiquities.
34. Letters in the Royal Archives, State Archives of Denmark.
35. The collection of antiquities together with acquisitions made by the Prince was finally on June 29th 1825 taken abord the corvette St. Croix, which had made a stop at Portici on its way to Copenhagen, Breitenstein 1951, 68.
36. Rasmussen 2006 and 2008,152-155.
37. Lund 2000.
38. Lund 2000, 131-132.
39. Rasmussen 2000.37-38.
40. Rasmussen 2006, 210-216.
41. Breitenstein 1951, Rasmussen & Lund 2004.
42. Birket Smith 1862, no.112.
43. CVA, Danemark fasc. 3, pl. 102, 2a-b.
44. Cf letter from J.D.Beazley to P.J.Riis in the archives of Col-

lection of Classical and Near Eastern Antiquities, National Museum of Denmark.

45. Letter from P.J.Riis to J.D.Beazley in the archives of Collection of Classical and Near Eastern Antiquities, National Museum of Denmark.

46. Report by Vivi-Ann Jacobsen August 9, 1966 in the Conservation department, National Museum of Denmark. Translation by the author.

47. Milnaese 2007.

48. Report by Ruth Frandsen in the Conservation Department, National Museum of Denmark. Translation by the author.

49. Snow 1986. Melander, 1984, 17-2 and 2000, 17, cat. 18.

50. Saunders & Svoboda 2012 and Svoboda 2013.

51. Steiner 2007, 212-215.

52. Madsen 1997, 85.